BRITISH NEWS UPDATE

6

Timothy Knowles
Minne Tanaka
Mihoko Nakamura
Sayaka Moue

JN125944

KINSEIDO

Kinseido Publishing Co., Ltd.
3-21 Kanda Jimbo-cho, Chiyoda-ku,
Tokyo 101-0051, Japan

BBC ニュース ホームページ：www.bbc.com/news

The British Broadcasting Corporation (BBC) is internationally famous for the quality and impartiality of its news items. BBC reporters also strive to make the news both interesting and as easy to understand as possible.

In this book we have chosen 15 items that we think would be of particular interest, and therefore motivating. Most of them are about Britain, as you might expect, and learners will gain an understanding of the life and culture of that country. As many of the issues covered are also important in Japan, there is the opportunity to discuss and compare the two countries. Japan itself is actually the focus of one item, which will provide an insight into the way the British view and report Japanese affairs. There is also an item about Antarctica, because of the international environmental importance of that area in the twenty-first century.

Sadly, 2022 saw the passing of Queen Elizabeth II, who had been on the throne of the United Kingdom and other Commonwealth countries for over 70 years. The first item of this volume shows the love and respect that the people felt for her.

As ever, new items of vocabulary are explained, and the notes (in Japanese) will explain any interesting points of grammar and usage of English. However, the most important purpose of this book is that the learners should be able to engage in the subject matter, research, and then discuss together. With this in mind, we have developed discussion questions that would encourage them to relate these new discoveries with what is already familiar to them.

The videos are easily accessible online. This will make it easy for students to study by themselves out of class.

We hope you enjoy the book and the videos.

はじめに

　本書は、実際に放送された BBC（英国放送協会）のニュースを教材として、ニュースキャスターや街頭インタビューを受ける native speaker が自然に話す英語に触れることで、学習者のリスニング力や語彙力といった英語力を伸ばすことを目的としています。同時に、イギリスや世界で起こっている出来事やその背景となる社会や文化についても学べるように工夫されています。

　扱うトピックは、政治、経済、環境などから、医療、人種、スポーツ、労働問題まで多岐にわたるものとし、できるだけ up to date でありつつも普遍的なものを選びました。学習する皆様の興味関心の幅を広げ、ご希望にお応えすることができれば幸いです。

　前作に引き続き、ユニット内のコラムは、イギリス文化についての興味深い情報を増やして充実を図り、Questions も最初の Setting the Scene に始まり Follow Up にいたるまで、各ユニットで取り上げるニュースを順序良く掘り下げて理解が深まるように配慮しました。

　本書を通じて、伝統と革新が共存する多民族国家イギリスが、4 つの地域の独自性を保ちつつ、総体としてのイギリスらしさ（"Britishness"）を模索する今の姿を見ていただけると思います。現在のイギリスは、新型コロナウイルスによる混乱は落ち着いたものの、70 年間にわたって国民を導いてきたエリザベス 2 世が崩御しチャールズ 3 世が新国王として即位するなど、新たな時代を迎えています。日本や世界に与える影響を考慮すると、今後もその動きから目が離せません。

　このテキストを使って学習する皆様が、イギリスや世界の状勢に興味を持ち、さらには、自分から英語ニュースに触れたり、英語で意見を述べたりと、ますます学習の場が広がっていきますことを、執筆者一同願っております。

　最後に、BBC ニュースを教材として使うことを許可してくださいました BBC、編集に際してご尽力いただきました金星堂の戸田浩平様に、この場をお借りして心より感謝申し上げます。

テキストの特徴

　普段の生活の中で、ニュースの英語に触れる機会はあまりないかもしれません。本テキストは、初めて英語でニュースを観る場合でも無理なく取り組めるよう、多種多様なアクティビティを用意しています。単語のチェックや内容確認、穴埋め、要約、ディスカッションを通して、段階を踏みながらニュースを理解できるような作りになっているので、達成感を感じることができるでしょう。

STARTING OFF
Setting the Scene

　実際にニュースを観る前に、ニュースで扱われるトピックについて考えるためのセクションです。トピックについての学習を始めるにあたり、身近な問題としてトピックを捉えられるような問題を用意しました。ここで先にニュースに関する情報を整理しておけば、実際にニュースを観る際に理解が容易になります。ニュースで使われている単語や語句、または重要な概念をここで予習しておきましょう。

Building Language

　ニュースの中で使われる重要単語を学びます。単に日本語の訳語を覚えるのではなく、英語での定義を通して、また同義語を覚えながら、単語の持つ意味を英語で理解することを目指します。また、これらの単語はディスカッションを行うときにもおそらく頻繁に使うことになる単語ですし、ニュースの核となる単語ですので、発音もしっかりと確認することが重要です。

WATCHING THE NEWS
Understanding Check 1

　実際にニュースの中身を詳しく見ていく前に、どんな意見が交わされているのかを確認します。ここで具体的にニュースのイメージをつかむことが大事です。全体像を簡単にでも把握することで、ニュース理解の大きな助けとなります。

Understanding Check 2

　ニュースに関する問題を解くことで、どれだけニュースを理解できたか確認することができます。間違えた箇所に関しては、なぜ間違えたのかをしっかりと分析し、内容を正確に把握しましょう。**Filling Gaps** のアクティビティを行ってから **Understanding Check 2** に取り組むのも効果的かもしれません。

Filling Gaps

ニュースの中で重要な意味を持つ単語を聞き取ります。何度も繰り返し聞き、正しい発音を意識します。それと同時に、単語を正しく書き取ることで、耳と手との両方の動きを通して重要単語を習得することを目指します。もし時間に余裕があれば、穴埋めの単語を実際に発音し、耳と手に加え口も使って覚えると効果的です。

MOVING ON

Making a Summary

この箇所は、これまで観てきたニュースをまとめる部分でもあり、かつ **Follow Up** に至る前の準備の段階でもあります。しっかりと内容を理解しているか、このアクティビティを通して確認しましょう。また、**Building Language** で出てきた単語を再度使っているため、単語の習熟の確認ができるようになっています。

Follow Up

ニュースと関連したトピックをいくつか挙げてあります。ニュースで得た知識、また単語を活かして話し合いを行うためのセクションです。トピックには、その場で話し合えるものと各自調べてから発表し合うもの、両方が含まれています。そのニュースに関してだけでなく、今後似たような話題に接したときにも意見を述べることができるよう、このアクティビティで仕上げを行います。

Background Information

ニュースでは、必ずしもすべての事柄が説明されているとは限りません。ニュースの核となる事柄で、かつニュースの中ではあまり詳しく説明されていないことに関して、このセクションでは補足しています。ニュースをより深く理解するのにも役立ちますし、**Follow Up** での話し合いの際にも使えるかもしれません。

Behind the Scenes

ニュースに関連することではありますが、**Background Information** とは異なりここではニュースの核となることではなく、話題が広がる知識、教養が深まる知識を取り上げました。肩の力を抜き、楽しんで読めるような内容になっています。

・各ユニットで取り上げたニュース映像はオンラインで視聴することができます。詳しくは巻末を参照ください。
・テキスト準拠の Audio CD には、各ユニットのニュース音声と、ニュースを学習用に聞き取りやすく吹き替えた音声、Making a Summary を収録しています。

Contents

Unit 1 Paying Respects to the Queen ················· 1
国民に愛された女王の葬儀　［2分44秒］

Unit 2 Music: The Key to Mental Health ··········· 7
DJ がもたらすメンタルヘルスへの効果　［2分52秒］

Unit 3 The London Olympic Park Today ··········· 13
オリンピックの遺産を未来へ　［3分30秒］

Unit 4 Prescriptions for Healthy Food ··········· 19
野菜の処方箋 !?　［2分43秒］

Unit 5 The Last British Maker of Ballet Shoes ·········· 25
危機に瀕するバレエシューズ　［2分33秒］

Unit 6 Nurses on Strike ······························ 31
看護師たちのストライキ　［2分53秒］

Unit 7 Sustainable Antarctic Cruises ··········· 37
南極クルーズで科学研究に貢献 !?　［2分58秒］

Unit 8 **The Wheelchair Rugby League World Cup** ⋯⋯⋯⋯⋯ 43
車いすラグビーのワールドカップ　［3分14秒］

Unit 9 **The First Female Mayor of Suginami** ⋯⋯⋯⋯⋯ 49
イギリスから見た日本の女性区長の苦悩　［3分37秒］

Unit 10 **Rescue of an Ancient Tavern** ⋯⋯⋯⋯⋯⋯⋯⋯ 55
中世の建築物の存続はいかに　［2分53秒］

Unit 11 **A New Treatment for Alzheimer's** ⋯⋯⋯⋯⋯⋯ 61
アルツハイマー病の新薬が登場！　［4分44秒］

Unit 12 **Liverpool's Slavery Heritage** ⋯⋯⋯⋯⋯⋯⋯⋯ 67
真の歴史を見据える都市リヴァプール　［2分46秒］

Unit 13 **New Businesses in Sunderland** ⋯⋯⋯⋯⋯⋯⋯ 73
起業で目指すサンダーランドの町おこし　［2分42秒］

Unit 14 **Brexit: How Do We Feel Now?** ⋯⋯⋯⋯⋯⋯⋯ 79
EU 離脱後の市民の葛藤　［3分27秒］

Unit 15 **Genomes of All Life in the British Isles** ⋯⋯⋯⋯ 85
すべての生物のゲノム解析を！　［3分09秒］

Map of The United Kingdom

正式名称は **The United Kingdom of Great Britain and Northern Ireland**（グレートブリテン及び北アイルランド連合王国）。**England**（イングランド）、**Wales**（ウェールズ）、**Scotland**（スコットランド）、**Northern Ireland**（北アイルランド）の4国から成る連合国家です（2023年現在）。

※（　）は本テキストでその地名、場所が登場するユニットを表します

North Atlantic Ocean

Greater London

Scotland

- Inverness

North Sea

Glasgow
Edinburgh

Hackney (Unit 5)
the Queen Elizabeth Olympic Park (the Olympic Park) (Unit 3, 8)
the Palace of Westminster (Unit 1)
the London Eye (Unit 1)
Stratford (Unit 3)
Lambeth Bridge (Unit 1)
River Thames
Tower Hamlets (Unit 4)
Lambeth (Unit 4, 6)
Brixton (Unit 4)
Tower Bridge (Unit 1)

Northern Ireland

Newcastle (upon Tyne) ● **Sunderland** (Unit 13)

Belfast

Isle of Man

York

Irish Sea

Lancashire (Unit 12)
Liverpool (Unit 12)
Manchester

Ireland

Conwy

England

Wales

Birmingham

Cardiff

Stratford-upon-Avon (Unit 14)
Oxford
Cambridge

Bristol
Bristol (Unit 12)

Windsor Castle (Unit 10)
Eton (Unit 10)
Surrey (Unit 11)
Brighton (Unit 2)
Dartford (Unit 8)
Dover

Portsmouth
Isle of Wight
Eastbourne (Unit 2)

St. Ives
Plymouth (Unit 15)

Unit 1

Paying Respects to the Queen

2022年、エリザベス女王が崩御しました。国葬に先立ち、女王を愛した多くのイギリス国民にも哀悼の意を表す機会が与えられました。その様子を見てみましょう。

On Air Date   12 September 2022

STARTING OFF

Setting the Scene

What do you think?

1. Can you remember when Queen Elizabeth II passed away? How old was she, and what took place in London eleven days later?

2. How many people do you think attended her funeral?

3. Did you watch the funeral on television? If you had been in the UK, would you have gone to London?

Building Language

For each word (1-6) find two synonyms (a-l).

1. dwarf [   ][   ]
2. mourn [   ][   ]
3. massive [   ][   ]
4. scent [   ][   ]
5. file [   ][   ]
6. coffin [   ][   ]

a. overshadow		g. parade	
b. huge		h. gigantic	
c. casket		i. box	
d. odour		j. walk	
e. minimise		k. smell	
f. regret		l. lament	

Understanding Check 1

Read the quotes, then watch the news and match them to the right people.

a. Our part is to say last goodbye, which is really sad.

b. And are you prepared to be in those, what are going to be very long queues?

c. … but we have been preparing for many, many years.

d. … I've got to do it. I feel that's my duty to do it.

( )   ( )   ( )   ( )

Understanding Check 2

Which is the best answer?

1. Lots of people queued to pay their respects to the Queen. Regarding those queues, which of the following is <u>not</u> correct?

  a. Mourners had to dress respectfully.

  b. Cameras and flowers were not allowed.

  c. If the lines were long, people were told to move faster.

  d. People might have had to wait overnight.

2. Maria, Vanessa, Amanda, and Moira gave us their reasons for being there. Which one of the following was <u>not</u> mentioned by any of them?

  a. They wanted to be part of it.

  b. The Queen served the country for 70 years.

  c. It was their duty.

  d. It was an important historical event.

3. Which of the following is a correct description of some of the route of the queue?

  a. Start near Tower Bridge, go up the Thames, and across Westminster Bridge.

  b. Go up the Thames, past Westminster Palace, then cross London Bridge.

  c. Start at Tower Bridge, pass the Palace of London, then cross Lambeth Bridge.

  d. Walk up the Thames, past the London Eye, then cross Lambeth Bridge.

What do you remember?

4. Until the Queen's lying-in-state began, where was 'home' for Vanessa? Why?

_____

5. What did Amanda and Moira say when asked if they were prepared to be in such long queues?

_____

6. Why was this day personally important for Commissioner Rowley?

_____

Background Information

　2022 年 9 月 8 日、イギリスの元首だった女王エリザベス 2 世（Elizabeth II, 1926-2022）が享年 96 歳で崩御しました。1952 年 2 月にジョージ 6 世（George VI, 1895-1952）が崩御するとすぐ、当時 25 歳だった娘のエリザベスはその責務を負って準備を進め、翌年 6 月に戴冠式が執り行われました。以来、常に真摯にその務めに向き合ってきた女王は多くの国民に愛され、2022 年 6 月には在位 70 年を祝うプラチナ・ジュビリー（Platinum Jubilee）が 4 日間にわたり盛大に開催されました。近年では息子のチャールズ 3 世（Charles III, 1948-　）現国王に公務を任せることが増えてきていた女王も、バッキンガム宮殿（Buckingham Palace）のバルコニーに姿を現し、イギリス歴代の君主で最長となった在位期間を祝いました。

　女王の国葬は 9 月 19 日に執り行われることとなり、準備が進められました。棺は女王が亡くなったスコットランドのバルモラル城（Balmoral Castle）からロンドンに移送された後、ウェストミンスターの議会議事堂内のホールに安置され、約 25 万人が弔問に訪れました。国葬には、日本の天皇・皇后両陛下、アメリカのジョー・バイデン大統領（Joe Biden, 1942-　）をはじめとする海外の要人約 500 人を含む約 2,000 人が参列し、雨の中、沿道を埋め尽くすほどの多くの市民が女王の棺を見送りました。ウェストミンスター寺院（Westminster Abbey）での国葬後、棺はロンドン郊外のウィンザー城（Windsor Castle）に運ばれ、歴代君主が眠る聖ジョージ礼拝堂（St George's Chapel）に埋葬されました。

　女王の死後、葬儀までの 10 日間、国中が喪に服して荘厳な儀式が続きました。実は式次第は 1970 年代にはすでに起草されており、女王自身が目を通し、細部には本人の希望も織り込まれていたのです。ロンドン滞在中や外国訪問中の崩御など、様々な想定のもとに多くの案が作成されていましたが、女王がスコットランド滞在中に死去した場合の「オペレーション・ユニコーン（Operation Unicorn）」と命名された案が実行されました。弔問のために棺の安置されたウェストミンスター寺院や、国葬、その後のウィンザー城への葬列では、近衛兵やさまざまな軍の部隊による護衛や行進が世界中に放映されました。

参考：
https://www.theguardian.com/commentisfree/2022/sep/19/the-guardian-view-on-the-queens-funeral-stirring-emotions-that-transcend-logic
https://www.theguardian.com/uk-news/2022/sep/08/queen-elizabeth-ii-obituary
https://www.royal.uk/platinumjubilee
https://www.theguardian.com/uk-news/2022/sep/08/operation-unicorn-plans-if-queen-dies-scotland

Filling Gaps

Watch the news, then fill the gaps in the text.

Lucy Manning: If you can measure love and respect in flowers, in people, then this is quite a statement. London's Green Park, now the park of many colours. The powerful (¹   ) of flowers, hanging in the air. But however many are here now will be (²   ) by the numbers who will stand, in a very British way, for hours and hours through the days and nights to
5 (³   ) past the Queen's (⁴   ).

Manning: People who do make it to Westminster Hall, where the Queen's body will lie in state, have been told to expect very long queues. The fear is they could last up to 24 hours, and (⁵   ) have been warned they may have to
10 wait overnight. If the lines are too long, they could be (⁶   ) so that people are unable to join. People have been asked to dress (⁷   ): no flowers, cameras, or filming allowed. Camping out on The Mall since Saturday, Maria from Newcastle plans to stay for the lying-in-state and funeral.

Maria Scott: She gave 70 years of (⁸   ) to us and it's the least I could
15 do to er, go and pay my respects to the Queen. She done so much for us, um, as a country, it's, you know, I've got to do it. I feel that's my duty to do it.

Manning: Vanessa Nanthakumaran hopes to be the first in the queue. Home, a bench on Lambeth Bridge until they open the doors.

20 **Vanessa Nanthakumaran:** Our part is to say last goodbye, which is really sad. But, um, I wanted to (⁹   ) (¹⁰   ) that I would be part of it, and start queuing up from today, um, because
25 I heard the queue's going to be very long.

Manning: More details on the (¹¹   ) for the queue are due shortly, but it's likely to begin near a park by Tower Bridge and travel a couple of miles up the Thames, passing the London Eye and the Palace of Westminster, then across Lambeth Bridge.

30 **Amanda:** And the smell is just incredible.

Manning: Amanda and Moira came to lay flowers but hope to return for the lying-in-state.

Moira: I think it's a once in a (¹²   ). You just want to be part of it.

Manning: And are you prepared to be in those, what are going to be very long queues?

Moira: Ah, well, there's the thing.

Amanda: Well, we're made of (¹³) stuff. So, we'll put it to the test. We'll put it to the test.

Moira: Yes. So, hopefully, yes. Yeah. Yeah, we would (¹⁴) it a (¹⁵).

Manning: It will be an (¹⁶) operation for the transport system and the police. The Met's commissioner on his first day in the job.

Sir Mark Rowley, Commissioner of Police of the Metropolis: It's a (¹⁷) challenge for the Metropolitan Police and for me personally, but we have been preparing for many, many years.

Manning: This ceremony will soon be (¹⁸) with simplicity, as the quiet walk past the Queen's (¹⁹) begins.

35

40

45

50

Notes

ℓ2 **Green Park**「グリーンパーク」王立公園の1つで、バッキンガム宮殿の北側に位置し、40 エーカー（16 ヘクタール）の広さがある。花がほぼ植えられておらず、樹木や芝の公園として知られている　ℓ7 **Westminster Hall**「ウェストミンスター・ホール」イギリス国会議事堂であるウェストミンスター宮殿にある大ホール。2022 年 9 月 14 日から 19 日の国葬までの間、女王の棺が安置され、一般弔問を受け付けた　ℓ12 **The Mall**「ザ・マル」バッキンガム宮殿とトラファルガー広場を結ぶ 930 m ある並木通り。儀式用の道路として 19 世紀後半から 20 世紀前半に作られた　ℓ13 **Newcastle**「ニューカッスル」イングランド北部タイン・アンド・ウィア州の港湾都市　ℓ19 **Lambeth Bridge**「ランベス橋」ロンドンのテムズ川に架かる橋で、北側のウェストミンスターと南側のランベスを繋いでいる。橋脚は貴族院のベンチの色と同じ赤に塗られている。現在の橋は 1932 年に開通した　ℓ27 **Tower Bridge**「タワーブリッジ」テムズ川にかかる橋桁が跳ね上がる跳開橋。1894 年に開通　ℓ28 **the London Eye**「ロンドン・アイ」テムズ川南岸のサウスバンクにある大観覧車。イギリスの 2000 年記念事業により 1999 年に開業した　ℓ28 **the Palace of Westminster**「ウェストミンスター宮殿」ロンドン中心部のテムズ川河畔にある宮殿。11 世紀半ばに王宮として建てられたが、1834 年の火災で大半が焼失し、1860 年に現在の建物が完成した。現在は英国議会が国会議事堂として使用している　ℓ45 **The Met's commissioner**「ロンドン警視庁の警視総監」正式名称は the Commissioner of Police of the Metropolis　ℓ47 **the Metropolitan Police (Service)**「ロンドン警視庁」イギリスの警察組織の1つで、大ロンドン一帯を管轄するとともに、王族や政府要人の警護の任務も担う。初代本部があった場所に因んでスコットランドヤード（Scotland Yard）とも呼ばれている

イギリス国歌の歌詞変更

　　イギリスの国歌はジョージ2世（George II，在位 1727-1760）治下の 1745 年に公の場で初めて演奏されて以来、現在まで同じ曲が使われていますが、実は1つの曲に対してタイトルや歌詞が2通りずつあり、君主が男性か女性かで使い分けています。これまでのエリザベス2世在位の約 70 年間、国歌のタイトルは「神よ女王を守り給え」（"God Save the Queen"）でしたが、この度のチャールズ3世の戴冠以後は「神よ国王を守り給え」（"God Save the King"）に変わりました。また、歌詞に出てくる代名詞も「彼女」「彼女の」（she, her）から「彼」「彼の」（he, his, him）に変更されました。これまでに女王版の国歌が歌われたのはヴィクトリア女王（Queen Victoria，在位 1837-1901）とエリザベス2世の時代のみですが、どちらも在位が長かったため、合計で 130 年を超える期間使用されたことになります。一方、男性版の国歌も合計で 140 年以上使われていますが、女王と比べて男性国王の変遷は激しく、チャールズ現国王で9人目です。

MOVING ON

Making a Summary

Fill the gaps to complete the summary.

　　The Queen has passed away and soon her body will lie in state in Westminster Hall. There are many people in Green Park, with the (**s**　　　　　) of flowers in the air. But that number of people will soon be (**d**　　　　　) by the number of (**m**　　　　　) who will queue for hours, and (**f**　　　　　) past the Queen's (**c**　　　　　) to pay their (**r**　　　　　). They might even have to wait overnight. They have been asked to dress (**r**　　　　　), and no flowers or cameras are allowed. Maria feels it is her duty to do it, as the Queen gave 70 years of (**s**　　　　　) to the country. Vanessa is staying on a bench on Lambeth Bridge because she wants to be first in the queue. Amanda and Moira say they are prepared for the wait, as they're made of strong (**s**　　　　　). According to the Commissioner of Police of the Metropolis, the event will be a (**m**　　　　　) challenge, and also important to him personally, as it is his first day on the job.

Follow Up

Discuss, write or present.

1. Are you surprised that people would queue for so long? What do you think were the most important reasons?

2. Can you think of anybody else who is (or was) respected as much as the Queen was respected by those people?

3. In what other ways do we show respect for people who have died, and want to remember them?

Unit 2

Music: The Key to Mental Health

世界的に有名な DJ が、メンタルヘルスの問題を持つ人たちに向けてワークショップを行っています。一体どのような取り組みなのでしょうか。ニュースを見てみましょう。

On Air Date   21 June 2022

STARTING OFF

Setting the Scene

What do you think?

1. Whenever you feel a bit miserable, what do you do to cheer yourself up?

2. If a friend of yours was feeling very unhappy, how would you help them? What advice might you give?

3. Fatboy Slim is a modern DJ. What does a DJ do?

Building Language

Which word or phrase (1-6) best fits which explanation (a-f)?

1. tremendously   [   ]
2. gig   [   ]
3. stigma   [   ]
4. fade   [   ]
5. renowned   [   ]
6. take for granted   [   ]

a. a musical performance, or other professional stage engagement

b. a great deal; to an extraordinary degree

c. well-known; famous

d. a mark of social disgrace, or damage to your reputation

e. accept the existence of something without thinking about it

f. become less bright (in light or colour), or quieter (in sound)

Understanding Check 1

Read the quotes, then watch the news and match them to the right people.

    a. Even though before I even got to the door, I stopped.

    b. The DJ has been honest about his own mental health struggles …

    c. It was joyous being involved in this workshop …

    d. I've been in psychiatric hospitals at, at parts of my life.

(   )   (   )   (   )   (   )

Understanding Check 2

Which is the best answer?

1. What is the main purpose of this workshop?

    a. to train people to become successful professional DJs

    b. to help people overcome mental health problems through playing music

    c. to raise money for mental hospital care

    d. to relax by escaping from music and dance and flashing lights

2. Which of the following was <u>not</u> mentioned by Amber or Jess?

    a. We should not be ashamed of our mental health problems.

    b. Being a DJ proves that I can step out of my everyday routine.

    c. Next time I'll forget my anxiety and push myself.

    d. We hope to have successful careers as DJs.

3. What is Jess going to do now?

    a. She's going to get herself a DJ deck.

    b. She's going to train to become a DJ.

    c. She's going to work with more DJs.

    d. She's going to dream about becoming a DJ.

What do you remember?

4. In what way has music helped Fatboy Slim?

_____

5. Why did Fatboy Slim feel that this workshop was so joyous?

_____

6. What do the organisers hope that other mental health services will do?

_____

Background Information

　ファットボーイ・スリム（Fatboy Slim）は、イギリスのクラブ DJ かつミュージシャンで、本名ノーマン・クック（Norman Cook, 1963-　）のいくつかある芸名やプロジェクトの１つです。ケント州ブロムリー（Bromley）に生まれ、大学入学以来ブライトンに移り、この海辺の保養地を拠点として音楽と DJ の活動を行っており、ロック、ハウス、テクノなど、さまざまなジャンルでヒット曲を多数出しています。

　ニュースで取り上げられているのは、国民保健サービス（NHS: National Health Service）の基金で運営されている慈善団体ヘッズ・オン（Heads On）が出資しているプロジェクトで、深刻なメンタルヘルスの問題を抱えている人々のためのアートのイベントを 2022 年に開催しました。今回のクックのイベントには、6 人の音楽好きの人々が参加し、他にも歌唱のワークショップやサンバ教室、サウンド・ヒーリングが行われました。このプロジェクトを主催したサセックス・パートナーシップ（Sussex Partnership）は大学病院連盟（University Hospital Association）の一員で、特にメンタルヘルスの面で地域の臨床医療と研究を促進する活動を行っています。

　メンタル面での健康維持の困難に直面しているアーティストは少なくありませんが、2020 年と 2021 年には新型コロナウイルスが猛威を振るい、音楽や演劇などのパフォーミング・アーツ業界はとりわけ大きな痛手を被りました。そのような状況を見て主催者側がクックに打診し、今回のイベントの開催が決定しました。音楽の配信をしたり、所有するカフェでウェイターをしたりしながらロックダウン期間を乗り切ったクックは、ライブの再開で忙しい中、若手の支援に励んでいます。自身もアルコール依存症を経験するなどしてメンタルヘルスの維持に関心を抱いていたクックは、音楽を通して病気を抱える人々の手助けができることを喜んでいます。パンデミックの終息に光が見え始めた今、アートの癒しの力が必要とされています。

参考：
https://www.theguardian.com/music/2022/jun/21/twiddle-knob-make-a-face-norman-cook-fatboy-slim-mental-health-dj-classes
https://www.theguardian.com/commentisfree/2017/apr/30/the-guardian-view-on-the-1997-labour-landslide-not-what-it-seemed
https://www.theguardian.com/society/2022/may/12/performing-arts-depression-equity-covid-job-insecurity

Filling Gaps

Watch the news, then fill the gaps in the text.

Newsreader: The world-(¹   ) DJ, Fatboy Slim, is staging a
    (²   ) with a difference, as part of a project to help people with
    severe mental health problems. The DJ has been honest about his own mental
    health struggles and the important part he feels music can play in helping

5   people (³   ). Clara Rackham reports.

Norman Quentin Cook: 1, 2, 3, 4.

Annabel Rackham: Is music the key to helping your mental health? At this
    (⁴   ) in Brighton, Norman Cook, better known as Fatboy Slim, is
    teaching DJ first timers about the (⁵   ) music can make.

10 **Cook:** That's it. Bang on.

Cook: Music's helped me
    (⁶   ) during my own
    mental health journey. As a DJ, what
    I try and do is help people escape.

15 And sometimes, it's good to escape
    your life or your stress for a couple
    of hours. And I've always done that
    for a living. But then, at times in my life, when things have been falling
    (⁷   ), I find that I'm doing it to myself as much as everybody. I

20 need those two hours where I just lose myself to music and dance and flashing
    lights. And it's a very (⁸   ) kind of therapy for me.

Rackham: Everyone here is recovering from (⁹   ) mental health
    problems and have spent a lot of time in hospital.

Jess: I'm Jess. I'm a drummer. And I'm from Brighton.

25 **Amber:** I'm Amber. I'm 26. And I am from Eastbourne, and I love to sing.

Jess: I've been in dark places pre- and post-COVID. I think that there's a lot of
    (¹⁰   ) attached to mental health that needs to not be there so
    much. I've been in psychiatric hospitals at, at parts of my life. But I don't think
    it's something to be (¹¹   ) of anymore.

30 **Cook:** All right. And that was bang on.

Amber: I was already on there and he came over.

Cook: Right, how are you doing?

Amber: I'm good. Thank you.

Amber: At first, I was just doing the (¹²   ) in and out. Then, he got me on the reverb and changing the pitch. Doing something like this, it just proves to me I can step outside of my everyday (¹³   ). Even though before I even got to the door, I stopped. Amber, can you actually do this? Anxiety just (¹⁴   ). The feeling I feel now will mean that I will push myself next time.

Cook: It was joyous being involved in this workshop because the people hadn't ever seen or touched decks before. I kind of (¹⁵   ) it (¹⁶   ) (¹⁷   ) because they're the tools of my trade. But seeing someone go, "woo, we can do that", it's a beautiful thing.

Amber: There's a lot to it. Isn't there?

Cook: I know, yeah.

Rackham: The organisers hope other mental health services in the UK can find (¹⁸   ) for more music workshops like this.

Cook: Can you hear that too? (¹⁹   )!

Rackham: And what about the chance to work with one of the world's best DJs?

Jess: It's just (²⁰   ). It's like a dream come true.

Amber: It's now pushed me to go and get myself a DJ deck.

Rackham: Annabel Rackham, BBC News, Brighton.

35

40

45

50

55

Notes

ℓ1 **Fatboy Slim** 「ファットボーイ・スリム」イギリスの DJ 兼ミュージシャンであるノーマン・クエンティン・クック (Norman Quentin Cook, 1963-) の数あるアーティスト名の1つ　ℓ5 **Clara Rackham** 「クララ・ラッカム」アナベル・ラッカム (Annabel Rackham) の誤り　ℓ8 **Brighton** 「ブライトン」イングランド南東部イースト・サセックス州にある都市。イギリス海峡に面しており、イギリス有数のリゾート地として有名である　ℓ25 **Eastbourne** 「イーストボーン」イングランド南東部イースト・サセックス州にある都市

DJ の語源

DJ とはディスクジョッキー (disc jockey) の略称です。ディスクジョッキーという言葉が初めて使われたのは 1941 年で、アメリカの娯楽業界誌『バラエティ』(*Variety*) の誌面上であったと言われています。ディスク (disc) は音楽を記録する円盤状の「レコード」を、ジョッキー (jockey) は馬を操る「騎手」を意味します。もとはラジオ放送の際に選曲した音楽を紹介してレコードをかける人のことを指していましたが、その後、録音された音楽を聴衆のために流す人のことを広く表すようになりました。ナイトクラブやフェスなどで活躍するクラブ DJ の元祖として知られるのはニューヨークのフランシス・グラッソ (Francis Grasso, 1948-2001) で、1960 年代、2 台のプレーヤーを使って曲同士のテンポとビートを合わせて途切れさせずに繋ぐ「ビートマッチング (beatmatching)」の技を編み出しました。

MOVING ON

Making a Summary

 CD 1-07

Fill the gaps to complete the summary.

The (r   ) DJ, Fatboy Slim, has helped to launch a workshop in which people with severe mental health problems can learn the skills of being a DJ. He is staging this (g   ) because he has struggled with mental health himself, and feels that music helped him (t   ). He thinks it's good to escape stress for a couple of hours, and when he is working, he can lose himself to music and dance and flashing lights. Amber, a singer, described how she could leave her everyday routine by performing as a DJ: for example, (f   ) in and out, doing the (r   ), and changing the (p   ). Anxiety used to overtake her, but now she feels she will push herself. Jess, a drummer, mentioned the (s   ) attached to mental health, which is nothing to be (a   ) of any more. Fatboy Slim found it joyous being involved, with participants using, for the first time, tools that he took for (g   ), and the organisers hope other UK health services can fund similar workshops.

Follow Up

Discuss, write or present.

1. Many people say music makes them happy, but being a DJ means playing music for others. Do you think being a DJ would cheer you up if you were miserable?

2. Listen to Fatboy Slim on https://www.youtube.com/watch?v=OOxWQ9CF-y4
   How would you describe his music? What do you think of it? Would it cheer you up?

3. Jess talked about the stigma attached to mental health. What did she mean? And do you agree with her that it is not something to be ashamed of?

Unit 3

The London Olympic Park Today

ロンドンでは 2012 年にオリンピックが成功裡に開催されましたが、その跡地は現在どのように活用されているのでしょうか。ニュースを見てみましょう。

On Air Date   21 July 2022

STARTING OFF

Setting the Scene

What do you think?

1. The 2020 Olympics were held in Tokyo. What can you remember about them?

2. Can you remember where the 2016 Olympics were held? What about the 2012 Olympics? What can you remember about them?

3. What do you think should happen to all the Olympic sites when the Olympics have ended?

Building Language

Which word or phrase (1-8) best fits which explanation (a-h)?

1. brownfield   [   ]
2. biodiversity   [   ]
3. haven   [   ]
4. enviable   [   ]
5. thrive   [   ]
6. rejuvenate   [   ]
7. white elephant [   ]
8. legacy   [   ]

a. something that is left behind after someone dies, or an event ends

b. make young again, or restore to an original, healthy state

c. desirable: something that other people wish that they had

d. a wide variety of living things in a particular area

e. land where there used to be industry, and now might be polluted

f. prosper, succeed and do very well

g. something that was very expensive to create, but later became worthless

h. a safe place where we can relax

Understanding Check 1

Read the quotes, then watch the news and match them to the right people.

a. ... they don't want a string of unused venues anymore ...

b. Children come with their teachers to learn about the site.

c. ... Stratford became one of the country's most environmentally-friendly areas.

d. ... and now we are sort of extending that interest throughout the year ...

( )   ( )   ( )   ( )

Understanding Check 2

Which is the best answer?

1. According to Ruth (the first woman), what is the present policy for the 2012 Gardens?

  a. Lots of visibly interesting structures are being built.

  b. The gardens should look spectacular for two weeks every year.

  c. Spaces should be created that change seasonally through the year.

  d. The number of hotels where people feel intimate are being increased.

2. What is it that the Olympics Committee don't want?

  a. crowds of tourists who want to see the Olympic stadium

  b. transport within the park

  c. lots of venues that are only used for the Olympics, and then not used again

  d. too many animals and plants

3. What plan did the Olympics Committee have for the concourses?

  a. They wanted to make the concourses smaller.

  b. They needed to keep the concourses to move people around.

  c. They planned to build temporary venues on the concourses.

  d. They wanted to plant laurels on them, to make a place for resting.

What do you remember?

4. What did the site look like before the Olympics?

_____

5. According to Victoria (the second woman), how did London win the bid for the 2012 Olympics?

_____

6. What kind of legacy are the bosses of the park aiming for?

_____

Background Information

　2012 年夏のロンドン・オリンピックのメイン会場として使用されたオリンピック・パークは、2014 年 4 月、クイーン・エリザベス・オリンピック・パーク（Queen Elizabeth Olympic Park）と名を改めて全面的に開園しました。建設には大会前から通算して約 10 年の歳月と約 120 億ポンド（約 2 兆 1,600 億円、1 ポンド＝ 180 円）の費用がかけられ、その後もさらなる地域開発が進められています。

　オリンピック・パークが建設されたイーストロンドンは、かつては工場や倉庫が密集し、産業廃棄物によって河川や土壌が汚染され、所得の低い労働者や移民が暮らす貧しい地域でした。しかし、ロンドン・オリンピックの開催が 2005 年に決定すると、土地の再開発とそれに伴う雇用や住宅の増加、治安の向上や環境の改善などを通じた地域の活性化が本格的に推進され、地元住民への利益の還元が期待されるようになりました。

　実際、オリンピックを経て、パークとその周辺地域の景観は一変しました。約 560 エーカー（約 220 ヘクタール）の敷地内にはロンドン・スタジアム（London Stadium）を中心とするスポーツ施設だけでなく、中央を流れるリー川（the River Lea）沿いの湿地や牧草地を散策できる遊歩道など、自然を楽しめる環境が整えられています。また、選手村を改装したイースト・ヴィレッジ（East Village）などの住宅街の整備も進んでおり、2036 年までにパーク内に建設予定の 33,000 戸のうち 10,000 戸以上がすでに完成し、新たな住人を受け入れています。さらに、ビジネスの支援にも力が注がれており、新興企業の共同ワークスペースや大学のキャンパスが入ったヒア・イースト（Here East）等の施設が、起業家や発明家を育成する拠点として機能しつつあります。

　しかし、こうした輝かしい側面とは裏腹に、地元住民たちは期待していたほどの恩恵を受けられず、不満を募らせています。例えば、パークやその周辺に新しく建設された住宅の大半は中流以上の所得者や富裕層向けで、地元の平均所得者層が借りることのできる「手頃な（affordable）」住宅は実質 1 割程度とも言われています。環境の変化や新たな住民層の流入によって地域の「高級化（gentrification）」が進み、格差が広がりつつあります。

参考：
https://www.queenelizabetholympicpark.co.uk/
https://www.theguardian.com/uk-news/2014/apr/02/london-olympic-park-open-public
https://www.theguardian.com/uk-news/2022/jun/30/a-massive-betrayal-how-londons-olympic-legacy-was-sold-out
https://www.bbc.com/news/uk-england-london-62138346

Filling Gaps

Watch the news, then fill the gaps in the text.

Newsreader: It's not easy, cheap, or quick to turn a large (¹   ) site into a sustainable, (²   ) (³   ). But it was achieved for the London 2012 Games. As well as the Olympics and Paralympics creating unforgettable memories, a part of Stratford became one of the country's most
5   environmentally-friendly areas. And that's where our environment correspondent, Tom Edwards, has been.

Tom Edwards: Welcome to the Queen Elizabeth Olympic Park. In the bid for the 2012 Olympics, sustainability and (⁴   ) were at its heart. Len used to walk here before the Olympics arrived, when it was a huge
10   (⁵   ) site.

Len: Ten years later, we've not only got a brilliant, um, brilliant park, but now, I think what, what East London's got is an
15   (⁶   ) resource. Children come with their teachers to learn about the site. Animals and plants (⁷   ) in the area.

20 **Edwards:** This is what it looked like then. It was an industrial area and had many pollution problems. This is what it looks like now. Millions have been spent (⁸   ) waterways, sowing meadows, and creating this habitat for wildlife.

Ruth Lin Wong Holmes, Design Principal, London Legacy Development
25   **Corporation:** The original design of the 2012 Gardens was supposed to look absolutely (⁹   ) for the two weeks of the games. Um, and now we are sort of extending that interest throughout the year with what, where we're sitting now in the, um, South Plaza. Um, but yeah, the whole idea was to create those sort of spaces that change seasonally through the year. So, you'll have a
30   point where there'll be some interest because there's a beautiful seedhead or something else in the park which has a great structure and um, visibly interesting. And then other parts of the year, you'll have the planting grow up to create rooms that make you feel more (¹⁰   ) and, and surrounded by green.

Edwards: Sporting bodies like the Olympics Committee don't want

(¹¹   ) (¹²   ): they don't want a string of unused venues

anymore, like we have seen in the past. What they want is a (¹³   ).

And the (¹⁴   ) here is meant to be one of sustainable regeneration.

One challenge is transport within the park and making that carbon neutral.

The area has been used to demonstrate new clean technologies, like these

driverless buses we filmed five years ago.

Victoria Thorns, Sustainability Manager, London Legacy Development

Corporation: New BBC Studios,

which is where the Maida Vale,

um, site is (¹⁵   ) to.

Edwards: And the park is still

growing. The buildings here all

have to meet strict energy

(¹⁶   ) targets.

Thorns: We (¹⁷   ) the

bid on being the greenest games ever. And I think it's the games itself, in terms

of the venues, delivered on that, but they also delivered it in a way of not

having big concourses we had for the Games. There were big concourses needed

then to move all those people around. But the plan was always to shrink those

concourses down, get rid of the temporary venues. This was water polo

originally. One of the things that we can't and we shouldn't do is be

(¹⁸   ) on our laurels.

Edwards: Many challenges lie ahead at the park, but bosses here are working to

make it a (¹⁹   ) of (²⁰   ) and sustainability. Tom

Edwards, BBC London.

Notes

ℓ 4 **Stratford** 「ストラトフォード」ロンドン東部のニューアム・ロンドン特別区にある地区の１つ ℓ 24 **London Legacy Development Corporation** 「ロンドンレガシー開発公社」ロンドン・オリンピックを機としてオリンピック・パークと周辺地域の開発を行っている公社。2012 年 4 月設立 ℓ 25 **the 2012 Gardens** 「2012 ガーデンズ」クイーン・エリザベス・オリンピック・パーク内の庭園で、世界各地の植物が収集されている ℓ 28 **South Plaza** 「サウス・プラザ」クイーン・エリザベス・オリンピック・パーク内にある広場 ℓ 39 **carbon neutral** 「カーボン・ニュートラル」二酸化炭素をはじめとする温室効果ガスの排出量から森林などによる吸収量を差し引いて、合計を実質的にゼロにすること ℓ 44 **the Maida Vale**（**Studios**）「メイダヴェイル（スタジオ）」ロンドン中央部のウェストミンスター自治区にある裕福な住宅街メイダヴェイル地区にある BBC のスタジオ。ビートルズなど数多くのポップスターや BBC 交響楽団などの収録に使われてきた。2018 年に閉鎖が発表され、当初は 2022 年に移転の予定だったが、2025 年に延期されている

プラントハンターによる植物収集

16 世紀後半から 18 世紀にかけてヨーロッパの裕福な紳士の間で庭造りが趣味として広がると、貿易網や植民地の広がりとともに異国の珍しい植物を収集する人が増加しました。チャールズ 1 世（Charles I, 1600-49）が所有する庭園の管理人にも任命されたジョン・トラデスカント（John Tradescant the Elder, c. 1570-1638）と息子ジョン・トラデスカント（John Tradescant the Younger, 1608-1662）は、それぞれヨーロッパやアメリカなどに派遣され、チューリップなどの当時としては珍しい植物を収集しました。また、自らもプラントハンターで植物学者でもあったジョセフ・バンクス（Joseph Banks, 1743-1820）が 1773 年にキュー王立植物園（The Royal Botanic Gardens, Kew）の顧問に任命されると、世界各地に人員を派遣し、多様な植物がイギリスにもたらされました。組織化された植物園だけでなく、貴族、医者、商人、土地所有者など、様々な職種や階級の人々が世界中の珍しい植物の収集に乗り出し、イギリスの植物研究、園芸、造園が大いに発展しました。

MOVING ON

Making a Summary

 CD 1-10

Fill the gaps to complete the summary.

London won the bid to hold the 2012 Olympic Games because they aimed to be the greenest games ever. They were built on what was a polluted (**b**   ) site, which, by 2012, was turned into a sustainable, (**b**   ) (**h**   ). After the Olympics, the Olympics Committee did not rest on their (**l**   ). They did not want any (**w**   ) (**e**   ), with lots of unused buildings. Millions were spent (**r**   ) waterways and sowing meadows, to turn it into one of Britain's most environmentally friendly areas: an (**e**   ) resource where animals and plants (**t**   ). The large concourses were shrunk, temporary venues were removed, and gardens were created with spaces that change seasonally. Although there are still many challenges ahead, London is aiming now for a (**l**   ) of (**b**   ) and sustainability.

Follow Up

Discuss, write or present.

1. What do you think will be the legacy of the Tokyo Olympics?

2. What do you think of the Olympics? Do you think it is important to keep them, or are they a waste of resources?

3. A 'white elephant' is something (usually a building) that cost a lot of money, and although we thought it was going to be worth something, it is now worthless. Do you know of any 'white elephants' either in Japan, or elsewhere?

Unit 4

Prescriptions for Healthy Food

物価が高騰するロンドンで、健康的な食品が入手しづらくなることを懸念して、ある対策をとっている地域があります。どのような取り組みでしょうか。ニュースを見てみましょう。

On Air Date   8 December 2022

STARTING OFF

Setting the Scene

What do you think?

1. What is your diet? In other words, what do you generally eat every day?

2. Do you think your diet is healthy?

3. How much money do you spend on food? Try and calculate what percentage of your income is spent on food. Is it sometimes difficult to afford food?

Building Language

Which word (1-6) best fits which explanation (a-f)?

1. prescribe   [   ]

2. tackle   [   ]

3. portion   [   ]

4. obesity   [   ]

5. premature   [   ]

6. vulnerable   [   ]

a. too early; before the expected time

b. recommend or order the use of a drug or other treatment

c. an amount of food suitable for one person

d. the condition of being very overweight or fat

e. at risk of being physically or emotionally hurt

f. solve a problem; deal with a difficulty or obstacle

WATCHING THE NEWS

Understanding Check 1

Read the quotes, then watch the news and match them to the right people.

a. That voucher make a difference.

b. … like eating healthy fruits and vegetables every day …

c. We've got, er, a diet-related ill health crisis in the country at the moment.

d. It's absolutely freezing here in Brixton Market this morning …

( )　　　( )　　　( )　　　( )

Understanding Check 2

Which is the best answer?

1. In the UK, by how much is the price of fresh food increasing?
  a. more than 13%
  b. less than 13%
  c. It isn't increasing.
  d. about 13%

2. Which one of the following best describes Nicola?
  a. She buys plantain because it is half the price of other vegetables.
  b. Her voucher helps her to keep her diabetes under control.
  c. She doesn't feel strong enough to be able to manage through the day.
  d. Because she has hypertension, she doesn't have many choices.

3. How does a bad diet compare with smoking, and drinking alcohol?
  a. Eating badly is almost as bad as smoking too many cigarettes.
  b. Obesity can cause certain types of cancers, but it is not as harmful as alcohol.
  c. People who eat badly are also likely to drink too much alcohol.
  d. A bad diet causes more illness than smoking and alcohol combined.

What do you remember?

4. What are doctors and nurses in two London boroughs being allowed to do, and why?

_____

5. What are the Alexandra Rose Charity and A.T Beacon? What do they do?

_____

6. In what way is the cost of living a barrier to eating well?

_____

Background Information

　物価が高騰するイギリスでは、2022年9月の時点でおよそ5世帯中1世帯が食料不足を経験し、約1,000万人の成人と400万人の子供が、食事を抜き何も食べない日があるなど、規則的な食生活を送れずにいます。特に、低所得の世帯においては、生鮮食品などの健康に良いとされる食料を購入できず、栄養不足や肥満、糖尿病や高血圧等のリスクが増加しています。もともとイギリス国民の健康には懸念があり、2017年の調査によると、イングランドの成人の63%が太り気味で、27%が肥満です。また、肥満関連の病気によって国民保健サービス（NHS: National Health Service）に年間約60億ポンド（約1兆800億円）以上の負担がかかっており、国民の健康の維持が課題となっていました。

　こうした状況下で、「果物と野菜を処方箋に（Fruit & Veg on Prescription）」プロジェクトが2022年11月から12ヶ月間にわたって試験的に実施され、貧しい人々に生鮮食品の引換券が与えられました。同様の引換券の配布自体は、アレグザンドラ・ローズ・チャリティ（Alexandra Rose Charity）によって2014年から行われていましたが、今回は「社会的処方（social prescribing）」の仕組みが利用され、医師などが対象者に生鮮食品を「処方」する形式が採用されました。この社会的処方とは、医療処置や薬ではなく地域のコミュニティとのつながりを通じて患者の健康状態を改善する取り組みで、患者は地域でのボランティア活動やガーデニング、スポーツなどへの参加を処方されます。イングランドNHSは、貧富の差などがもたらす健康格差を解消すべく、個々の患者が自分に合った選択をして自身の健康を管理できるようになる「普遍的個別ケア（Universal Personalised Care）」を目指しており、その一環として社会的処方の普及に努めています。

　今回のプロジェクトは、ロンドンで最も貧しい地域であり慢性疾患を抱える人が多いとされるランベスとタワーハムレッツで実施されました。対象となった約120人の患者には1週間に最大8ポンド（約1,440円）分の野菜や果物が処方され、その家族にも1人あたり1週間に2ポンド（約360円）ずつの引換券が配布されました。試験運用の結果、食料不足の解消や患者の健康状態の改善に有用であると判断された場合には、対象地域を拡大し、より多くの貧しい人々を救済していく予定です。

参考：
https://www.bma.org.uk/media/2071/bma-improving-the-nation-s-diet.pdf
https://www.theguardian.com/society/2022/oct/18/millions-forced-to-skip-meals-as-uk-cost-of-living-crisis-deepens
https://www.alexandrarose.org.uk/press-release-fruit-and-veg-on-prescription-pilot-launched-to-tackle-ill-health-and-food-poverty/

Filling Gaps

Watch the news, then fill the gaps in the text.

Newsreader: GPs and nurses in two London boroughs are now allowed to
(^{1}) fruit and veg to patients. It's to see if it'll help
(^{2}) ill health and food poverty, and, er, the, the
(^{3}). Well, they're in the form of vouchers. Wendy Hurrell has
5   been to see how it works.

Wendy Hurrell: It's absolutely freezing here in Brixton Market this morning, and
as winter starts to bite, we're also thinking about food (^{4}), which
is at currently something like 13%, and for fresh stuff, even more than that. Er,
there's one charity that says the calories in unhealthy food is three times
10   cheaper than the healthier (^{5}), which is why here in Lambeth,
and also in Tower Hamlets, they're putting fruit and veg on (^{6})
to help people with their health.

Nicola: Black cabbage, please, a
(^{7}).

15 **Hurrell:** Like Nicola, for example.
She's trying to keep her
hypertension and type 2 diabetes
under (^{8}).

Nicola: Yeah. A (^{9}) of
20   cherries, like, maybe a pound …

Hurrell: So the last couple of months, her NHS nurse has given her vouchers for
healthy food, to exchange at (^{10}) market stalls, like Tracy's
one in Brixton.

Nicola: I'm a Jamaican, and I most, I bought my plantain, and that costs a pound
25   before and now it's two pounds. That voucher make a difference. So, that means
you, you, you have (^{11}), so it makes me feel younger, feel
stronger, feel healthy, and can able to manage through the day.

Woman: There you go.

Hurrell: Clear benefits for this hardworking mum, then. The (^{12}) is
30   run and funded by the Alexandra Rose Charity, which tries to
(^{13}) food poverty, and health inequality. Now, they've teamed up
with A.T Beacon, a like-minded project that gets healthcare to
(^{14}) communities.

Jonathan Pauling, CEO, Alexandra Rose Charity: We've got, er, a diet-related ill health crisis in the country at the moment. It's been around for a long time: um, er, (¹⁵   ), cardiovascular disease, certain types of cancers. A, a bad diet is responsible for more (¹⁶   ) deaths and illness than smoking and alcohol combined now. So, we've had this problem for a long time, but the cost-of-living crisis is just making it (¹⁷   ).

Dr Chi-Chi Ekhator, GP Lead, A.T Beacon: Simple (¹⁸   ), like eating healthy fruits and vegetables every day, which is absolutely possible, but we know that the cost of living, um, is a, is a (¹⁹   ). Er, but these small (²⁰   ) can improve people's lives and save the NHS millions.

Hurrell: So, central government has (²¹   ) support and the charities hope to reach more people like Nicola across London. Wendy Hurrell, BBC London.

Notes

ℓ1 **GPs**「総合診療医」general practitioners の略　ℓ6 **Brixton**「ブリクストン」ロンドン南部のランベス特別区にある地区　ℓ10 **Lambeth**「ランベス」大ロンドン中部テムズ川右岸の区　ℓ11 **Tower Hamlets**「タワーハムレッツ」大ロンドン東部の独立自治区　ℓ17 **type 2 diabetes**「2 型糖尿病」高血糖や糖尿が慢性的に続く代謝疾患。遺伝的な要因に加え、生活習慣の影響により発症すると言われている　ℓ21 **NHS**「国民保健サービス」the National Health Service の略。イギリスの国営医療サービス　ℓ24 **plantain**「料理用バナナ」　ℓ25 **That voucher make a difference**「あの引換券は違いを生み出します」正しくは That voucher makes a difference となる　ℓ34 **Alexandra Rose Charity**「アレグザンドラ・ローズ・チャリティ」1912 年に英国王エドワード 7 世 (Edward VII, 1841-1910) の妻でデンマーク出身のアレグザンドラ王妃 (Queen Alexandra, 1844-1925) によって設立された慈善団体。薔薇を売って貧しい人々を助けたデンマークのある神父に倣って、低所得家族に新鮮な食料品を支給することを目的として活動している　ℓ40 **A.T Beacon**「A・T・ビーコン」ロンドンの南東部で、健康に関する機会の不平等を是正することを目指す慈善団体

ジェイミー・オリヴァー（Jamie Oliver, 1975-　）は BBC で放送された料理番組『裸のシェフ』（*The Naked Chef*, 1999-2001）で一躍人気となった料理人ですが、学校給食の改革にも乗り出しました。2005 年に放送された『ジェイミーのスクール・ディナー』（*Jamie's School Dinners*）では、グリニッジのある学校において給食の質を上げるため、ジャンクフードの提供の禁止、調理師の教育、予算増加のための政治家への陳情を行いました。この放送をきっかけにイギリス全土で不健康な給食を改善しようという風潮が広がり、27 万人もの署名が集められ、当時のトニー・ブレア首相（Tony Blair, 1953-　）は学校給食の改善を約束するに至りました。その後オリヴァーはアメリカでの食生活改善にも取り組み、そうした活動が評価され、世界を鼓舞するアイデアを持つ人物に与えられる「TED プライズ（TED Prize）」を 2010 年に受賞しました。受賞講演「すべての子供に食育を」（"Teach every child about food"）は世界で反響を呼びました。

MOVING ON

Making a Summary

CD 1-13

Fill the gaps to complete the summary.

There has been a diet-related health crisis in Britain for a long time. Due to (**o**　　　　　　), cardiovascular disease, and cancer, a bad diet is responsible for more (**p**　　　　　　) deaths than smoking and alcohol combined. The cost-of-living crisis is making the situation worse, as 13% food inflation is forcing people to buy cheaper food, which is much more unhealthy. The Alexandra Rose Charity, which (**t**　　　　　　) food poverty and health inequality, has teamed up with the A.T Beacon Project, which gets healthcare to (**v**　　　　　　) people, to fund a scheme in which GPs and nurses can (**p**　　　　　　) fruit and vegetables to patients. Patients are given (**v**　　　　　　), which they exchange for (**p**　　　　　　) of fruit or vegetables. One example is Nicola, who uses her voucher to buy (**p**　　　　　　), which helps her to feel strong and healthy. The charities hope to reach more people like Nicola across London.

Follow Up

Discuss, write or present.

1. In Britain, food prices are increasing a lot. Why do you think food prices are increasing? Is the same thing happening in Japan? Give some examples.

2. Is there also a diet-related health crisis in Japan? Do people buy cheaper unhealthy food instead of more expensive healthy food?

3. Do you think the government should try to influence what we eat, or should we be able to eat what we like, even if it is unhealthy?

Unit 5

The Last British Maker of Ballet Shoes

古くからイギリスで製造され、世界中で愛されてきた ある伝統工芸品の存続が危ぶまれています。一体何が 起こっているのでしょうか。ニュースを見てみましょ う。

On Air Date   8 April 2022

STARTING OFF

■ Setting the Scene ■

What do you think?

1. Have you ever been interested in ballet dancing? What do you like, or dislike, about it?

2. Ballet dancers often stand high on their toes. Do you know how they do that? Could you do it?

3. If your shoes need to be repaired, do you just throw them away and buy a new pair, or do you take them somewhere to be repaired? If so, where do you take them?

■ Building Language ■

Which word or phrase (1-6) best fits which explanation (a-f)?

1. made-to-measure [   ]
2. tucked away [   ]
3. privilege [   ]
4. satin [   ]
5. bespoke [   ]
6. intangible [   ]

a. a benefit or right enjoyed by one person or a small group
b. specially made to fit a particular person
c. made privately, according to a customer's specifications
d. hidden
e. incapable of being touched, or being perceived by the sense of touch
f. a fabric such as nylon or silk made to have a smooth, glossy texture

Understanding Check 1

Read the quotes, then watch the news and match them to the right people.

a. It just makes it a lot stronger.

b. So, without the people that know them and have the skills to do them …

c. So really, it's a massive team effort.

d. … but there are fears that skill could be lost forever …

1 ( ) 2 ( ) 3 ( ) 4 ( )

Understanding Check 2

Which is the best answer?

1. What is special about Freed of London?
   a. They make more ballet pointe shoes than any other company.
   b. They are the only producer of ballet pointe shoes left in the UK.
   c. They are one of East London's biggest companies.
   d. People from all over the world are trained there.

2. Why does Ray think that making these shoes is a privilege?
   a. They are worn by a lot of famous people.
   b. The shoes are so good that dancers don't have to worry about them.
   c. He is very well paid.
   d. He can travel around the world training people.

3. How long have pointe shoes been made in London, and how many are produced there in a year now?
   a. They were made in 1900. More than a quarter of a million are produced.
   b. They've been made for almost a century, and fewer than 100,000 are produced.
   c. They've been made for nearly 100 years. More than 250,000 are produced.
   d. They've been made for many centuries, and millions are produced.

What do you remember?

4. Why does Sophie (the first woman) say that it is a massive team effort?

_____

5. What are people afraid of?

_____

6. What does Mary (the second woman) mean when she says that the skill of making pointe shoes is an intangible heritage?

_____

Background Information

　今回のニュースは、「伝統工芸レッドリスト (The Heritage Crafts Red List)」に「近絶滅種 (Critically Endangered)」として分類されたトウシューズ製作 (pointe shoe making) を取材しています。このリストは、伝統工芸の維持発展を目指して 2009 年に設立された伝統工芸協会 (The Heritage Crafts Association) が 2017 年より発表している継承が危ぶまれる伝統工芸のリストで、国際自然保護連合 (IUCN: International Union for the Conservation of Nature) が発表している生物の絶滅の危険度を表す「レッドリスト (Red List)」に倣って分類しています。伝統工芸を次の世代に継承するのに十分な人材がいる状態を「生存」している状態とみなし、危機に瀕している業種を「絶滅危惧種 (Endangered)」「近絶滅種 (Critically Endangered)」「絶滅種 (Extinct)」に分けています。

　フリード・オブ・ロンドン (Freed of London) は、現在、セミオーダーのトウシューズを手作業で製作しているイギリスで唯一のメーカーです。創設者フレデリック・フリード (Frederick Freed, 1899-1993?) はイーストロンドンに生まれた靴職人で、1929 年に妻と共にコヴェント・ガーデンのセシルコートに靴屋を開きました。当時は地下室で靴を制作していましたが、手狭になったため、1934 年に近くのエンデル・ストリートに製作所を移しました。1936 年には、王立となったロイヤル・アカデミー・オブ・ダンス (RAD: Royal Academy of Dance) との関係が始まり、1947 年に企業登記局 (Companies House) に登録すると、以後ますます成長していき、世界でも有数のトウシューズメーカーとしての地位を固めました。1968 年にフリード夫妻が引退してからは、レスターに本拠を置くダンスウェアを扱う会社の傘下に入りました。1971 年より製作の本部をハックニーのウェル・ストリートに移転し、1975 年にはニューヨークにもオフィスを開いて国際的な事業を展開していきます。1986 年には、日本のダンスウェアメーカーであるチャコットに買収され、1989 年には日本で 4 番目の小売企業であるオンワードの傘下に入っています。

　フリード・オブ・ロンドンは、バレエ学校やバレエ団と直接つながりを持ち、ダンサーのニーズに直に応えるトウシューズを一貫して製作してきました。2023 年の時点で、職人 28 人と見習い 3 人が在籍しています。事業は順調に見えましたが、新型コロナウイルスのパンデミックにより、舞台芸術の分野は大きな打撃を受け、トウシューズの需要が激減しました。その上、原材料の皮や絹のイギリス国内での供給が減ったため入手が困難になり、工芸の継承が危ぶまれています。

参考：
https://heritagecrafts.org.uk/redlist/categories-of-risk/
https://www.freedoflondon.com

Filling Gaps

Watch the news, then fill the gaps in the text..

Newsreader: Next, we are going to take you to the cobblers (¹   )
(²   ) in East London, who keep prima ballerinas on their toes.
Freed of London is the only producer of ballet pointe shoes left in the UK. Their
master (³   ) and women make their shoes by hand, up to 41 pairs
a day, but there are fears that skill could be lost forever, as Harry Lowe
explains.

Harry Lowe: Step inside this Hackney factory, and it doesn't take long to notice
the smells and sounds behind this (⁴   ) craft. The pointe
shoes created here end up being used by performers all over the world.

Ray Rawlins, Freed of London: And what this does is, it (⁵   ) the
block of the shoe for the dancer to stand up on. It just makes it a lot stronger.

Lowe: (⁶   ) (⁷   ) in the corner is one of the most
(⁸   ) shoe makers, Ray, who still works in the East End, where he
grew up.

Rawlins: It's a (⁹   ) to
know what you made is going on
stage and you know, a lot of times
dancers are more
(¹⁰   ) about what
they got to do and then what the
shoe, because if they know what
the shoes're like, then they just
got to worry about what they've got to do on stage.

Lowe: Ray is just one of the many (¹¹   ) of hands which go into
making the shoes worn by ballerinas from Brooklyn to Beijing.

Sophie Simpson, Freed of London: We make everything. We buy all our
(¹²   ) materials, so we produce the uppers, the (¹³   ) part,
we make all them bits that go into the block. We also make the soles. So really,
it's a massive team effort.

Lowe: Pointe shoes have been made in London for almost a century. And more than
a (¹⁴   ) of a million of them are produced here every year. Up to 25
people are involved in creating each (¹⁵   ) ballet shoe, but this
heritage craft is in danger of being lost to the UK.

28

Lowe: The Heritage Crafts Red List sets out skills which are (**16**   ) and Freed of London is the last British producer left. But in a globalised world, why is it important to keep hold of them?

Mary Lewis, Heritage Crafts Association: We believe that, er, our heritage craft skills are important cultural (**17**   ). There are, they are part of our living heritage and they're as important to us as, say our stately homes or our historic (**18**   ) and gardens and the art that we have on the walls. But these are things that are within people, so these are (**19**   ) heritage. So, without the people that know them and have the skills to do them, then they, they can't exist.

Lowe: Although Freed of London is (**20**   ) for now, they're not the only ones hoping they can keep dancers on their toes for generations to come. Harry Lowe, BBC London.

Notes

ℓ2 **East London** 「イーストロンドン」ロンドンの東部　ℓ3 **Freed of London** 「フリード・オブ・ロンドン」イングランド中部のレスター (Leicester) に本社を置くバレエシューズやダンスシューズの製造会社。1929 年設立。ロンドンのハックニーに主力工場がある　ℓ7 **Hackney** 「ハックニー」ロンドン中心部の北東部にある行政区　ℓ10 **block** 「ブロック」トウシューズの固いつま先　ℓ13 **the East End** 「イーストエンド」ロンドン東部にあり、古くから商工業地区として知られる地域　ℓ34 **The Heritage Crafts Red List** 「伝統工芸レッドリスト」継承が危ぶまれる伝統工芸のリスト。伝統工芸の維持発展を目指して 2009 年に設立された伝統工芸協会 (The Heritage Crafts Association) が 2017 年より発表している　ℓ43 **living heritage** 「生きている遺産」文化遺産の保護に関する議論において用いられる用語で、地域社会の中で有効に活用されている文化遺産を指す

　2023 年版「伝統工芸レッドリスト」では、手吹きによる板ガラス製作 (mouth-blown sheet glass making) が「絶滅危惧種」から「絶滅種」に更新されました。吹き竿 (blowpipe) の先端に溶けたガラスを付着させ、息を吹き込んで円筒形にしてから切り裂いて板状にする製法です。19 世紀初頭までの多くの窓ガラスはこの方法で作られた一点物で、気泡が入った独特の味わいを持っていました。20 世紀半ば以後、溶融した金属の上に溶けたガラスを浮かべて板状にするフロート法 (the float process) が誕生し、伝統の職人技は徐々に失われていきました。2022 年、バーミンガムのイングリッシュ・アンティーク・ガラス (English Antique Glass) という会社がこの技法での板ガラス製作を止めたことにより、イギリス国内では事実上の「絶滅」となりました。現在ではポーランドとドイツにわずかに製造業者が残っているのみです。

MOVING ON

Making a Summary

 CD 1-16

Fill the gaps to complete the summary.

　Freed of London is a company that produces (**b**　　　　　　) ballet pointe shoes. (**T**　　　　　) (**a**　　　　　　) in East London for almost a century, it is the only such producer left in the UK, with more than a quarter of a million shoes made each year. Their master craftsmen and women make them by hand, with up to 25 people involved in creating each (**m**　　　　　　) shoe. It is a (**m**　　　　　　) team effort, as they buy their own materials and make everything themselves, including the uppers, the soles, the blocks, and even the (**s**　　　　) part. Ray, one of the most experienced craftsmen, says that it is a (**p**　　　　) to know that he has made shoes that ballerinas need not worry about, so they can concentrate on their dancing. His skills are considered to be an (**i**　　　　　　) (**h**　　　　　) and an important cultural resource that we mustn't lose. The company is (**t**　　　　　) now, and it is hoped they will continue to do so.

Follow Up

Discuss, write or present.

1.　Take a look at the company's web page (https://www.freedoflondon.com). Does the company look as if it is thriving? What else does it make?

2.　Have you ever bought something 'made-to-measure'? If you could afford it, what clothing would you like made to measure?

3.　In the news, we heard about the importance of craft skills as important cultural resources. Does Japan have the same 'intangible heritage' that you want to keep?

Unit 6

Nurses on Strike

イギリスの看護師たちが路上で声を挙げ、待遇の改善を求めています。大規模なストライキの様子について、ニュースを見てみましょう。

On Air Date 6 February 2022

STARTING OFF

Setting the Scene

What do you think?

1. Do you know any nurses? What sort of job is it? Do they like their work?

2. How much do you think nurses should be paid? Do you think they are paid enough?

3. Do you think that nurses should be allowed to go on strike if they want to be paid more?

Building Language

Which word or phrase (1-8) best fits which explanation (a-h)?

1. walkout [ ]
2. in their droves [ ]
3. advocate [ ]
4. negotiation [ ]
5. engage in [ ]
6. constructive [ ]
7. disruption [ ]
8. dispute [ ]

a. working or talking with each other in order to reach an agreement
b. a strike or refusal to work by a number of workers
c. speak or write in support of a cause or idea
d. positive; helping to improve or develop
e. occupy yourself, or become involved in something
f. extreme disturbance or interruption
g. argument, debate, controversy, or difference of opinion
h. in a big crowd of people

WATCHING THE NEWS

Understanding Check 1

Read the quotes, then watch the news and match them to the right people.

   a. We don't get better care without more nurses …

   b. This has been the biggest nursing strike so far …

   c. I've been a nurse for a very long time …

   d. We have been inviting the government to come to the table …

(   )   (   )   (   )   (   )

Understanding Check 2

Which is the best answer?

1. Why are the nurses striking?
   a. They want a pay increase of 5%.
   b. They are not asking for a pay rise, but want better working conditions.
   c. They want a pay increase to be equal to inflation.
   d. They want an increase in salary of inflation plus 5%.

2. According to Charlotte (the last woman we talked to), what will the RCN do if there is an offer on the table?
   a. If the offer is not good enough, they will ignore it and continue the strike.
   b. If the offer meets them half-way, they will accept it.
   c. They will suspend the strike action and ask the nurses what they think about it.
   d. They will only stop the strike if they get the same offer as Scotland and Wales.

3. What should people do if they need urgent medical care during the strike?
   a. There are some disruptions, but they should still go to hospital.
   b. They have to wait at home until the strike is over.
   c. Everything is running as normal. They should telephone for an ambulance.
   d. Only chemotherapy and dialysis will be available.

What do you remember?

4. According to Sarah (the first woman we talked to), how have things changed since she started as a student?

_____

5. What reason did Malcolm (the man) give for nurses leaving the profession?

_____

6. What did the government's Health and Social Care Secretary say in his statement?

_____

Background Information

　イギリスでは国民の生活費が高騰し続けています。2022年7月のインフレ率は10.1%で、40年ぶりの高水準となりました。国民保健サービス（NHS: National Health Service）の看護師は政府から給与を得ていますが、2022年7月に発表された給与水準はインフレ率を下回りました。イングランドの看護師の平均年収は約32,000ポンド（約576万円）ですが、前年と比較して実質5,000ポンド（約90万円）減少しています。その結果、多くの看護師たちが離職したため、2022年9月時点で常勤の看護師約47,000人が不足し、欠員率は11.9%となりました。現場の看護師たちが人手不足と過重労働に苦しめられる中、2022年12月15日と20日、世界最大の看護師組合でありNHSの看護師の3分の2にあたる約30万人が所属している王立看護協会（RCN: Royal College of Nursing）が、設立106年の歴史で初めてイングランド、ウェールズ、北アイルランドにおいてストライキを行い、国に対してインフレ率に応じた19%の賃上げを求めました。

　スコットランドでは2022年12月には賃上げ案をRCN側が拒否していましたが、ストは回避され、その後2023年2月に投票を行い、給与案を受け入れる決議をし、看護師たちは給与額に応じて2023年に387ポンド（約7万円）から939ポンド（約17万円）を、そして2023年度に平均6.5%の賃上げを受け取ることになりました。その他の地域では、2023年に入ってもほぼ毎月ストが行われ、交渉が続きました。ウェールズでは2022年度の給与に3%上乗せした額の支払いと、2023年度における5%の昇給案が提示されましたが、RCNによって拒否されました。イングランドでは他より遅れて2023年3月16日に給与案が提示されたものの、RCNによって一度は拒否されました。北アイルランドでは2022年度の賃上げ額が支払われましたが、2023年度は予算不足のため賃上げが難しいと伝えられるなど、イギリス各地で交渉が難航しました。

　12月20日時点で、イングランドではストによって35,000件の手術と診療予約がキャンセルされました。しかし、一般市民の60%は看護師たちのストを支持しており、労働者たちの要求は正当なものだと考える人が多数います。また、看護師だけでなく、救急隊員、公共交通機関、郵便局、教職員、ごみの回収作業員など、様々な職種の人々による賃金上昇を求めるストも行われました。相次ぐストが市民生活に影響を及ぼす中、今後どのような決着が見られるのか、国民の注目が集まっています。

参考：
https://www.england.nhs.uk/2023/05/nhs-publishes-data-following-nurses-strike/
https://www.bbc.com/news/business-62134314

Filling Gaps

Watch the news, then fill the gaps in the text.

Newsreader: Nurses across the capital are on strike today. Nearly a dozen London hospitals are (^{1}) during what's thought to be the biggest (^{2}) in the capital so far. It's part of (^{3}) strike action by the Royal College of Nursing over pay and conditions. Our reporter,

5   Wendy Hurrell spoke to some of those on the picket line in South London.

Wendy Hurrell: Noisy support came (^{4}) from cars, buses, and ambulances passing by King's College Hospital in Lambeth this morning, from nurses on the picket line.

Nurses (*chanting*)**:** What do you want? Fair pay! When do you want it? Now! What

10   do you want? Fair pay!

Hurrell: It's a profession not usually (^{5}) with strike action.

Sarah Klyne, practice nurse educator, King's College Hospital: I've been a nurse for a very long time, and when I started as a student, it was not a thing that was going to happen, the union were dead against it. But things have got

15   so bad.

Laura Duffell, nurse, King's College Hospital: We're finding nurses leaving (^{6}) (^{7}) (^{8}), and it's gotten to, er, it's kind of gotten to a clinch point now, we just can't deal with it anymore. And, if we don't start speaking up, and (^{9}) for our patients, then, you

20   know, we're, kind of, we are not doing our jobs.

Nurses (*chanting*)**:** What do we want? Fair pay! When do we want it? Now!

Hurrell: The union is asking for a pay (^{10}) of inflation plus 5%, while also raising the voices of its members who are (^{11}) about staffing levels and patient safety.

25 **Malcolm Bennison, registered nurse:** We don't get better care without more nurses, and the reason, one of the many reasons nurses are leaving the profession is that pay isn't good enough.

Navneet Singh, clinical facilitator: I'm very proud to work in the NHS. I love the NHS, but we have to support it.

30 **Nurses** (*chanting*)**:** We need you to (^{12})!

Hurrell: The RCN says that since the first strike in December last year, there have been no formal pay (^{13}).

Charlotte Daus, regional officer, Royal College of Nursing: We have been inviting the government to come to the table and, um, put an offer, and we have said that we we'd be prepared to meet them half-way. And as, as is shown in Scotland and Wales, if an offer is brought to the table, we will (¹⁴   ) the strike action and put that offer to our membership.

Hurrell: No one from the government was available to talk to us today. We were given a (¹⁵   ) by Steve Barclay, the Health and Social Care Secretary, in which he says, it is time for the trade unions to look forward and (¹⁶   ) (¹⁷   ) a (¹⁸   ) dialogue about the Pay Review Body process for the coming year.

Hurrell: Of course, this does mean there has been (¹⁹   ) to patients today, with some treatments, operations, and appointments (²⁰   ). Er, but there is special cover for things like chemotherapy and dialysis, and there are nurses working in intensive care. The message still during these strikes is to go to hospital if you need (²¹   ) medical care. This has been the biggest nursing strike so far, in a (²²   ) that doesn't look like it's going to go away anytime soon. Wendy Hurrell, BBC London, at King's College Hospital.

35

40

45

50

55

Notes

ℓ4 **the Royal College of Nursing (RCN)**「王立看護協会」ロンドンを拠点とする看護専門職のための世界最大規模の労働組合。1916 年に設立された職能団体を基とし、1928 年に勅許を得た　ℓ5 **picket line**「ピケットライン」ストライキ中に屋外に設置される人々の集団。妨害者や脱落者の監視と阻止、他の労働者へのスト参加の促進、通行人へのアピールを行う　ℓ5 **South London**「サウスロンドン」ロンドンのテムズ川南部の地域　ℓ7 **King's College Hospital**「キングス・カレッジ病院」ロンドン南部のランベス自治区にある病院。研修医への医学教育を行う教育病院 (teaching hospital) で、外傷患者への緊急医療なども行っている。ロンドン北西部、現在のカムデン自治区にあたる地域で 1840 年に設立され、1909 年に現在の場所に移設された　ℓ7 **Lambeth**「ランベス」大ロンドン中部テムズ川右岸の区　ℓ28 **the NHS**「国民保健サービス」the National Health Service の略。イギリスの国営医療サービス　ℓ44 **Steve Barclay**「スティーヴ・バークレー (1972-)」イギリスの保守党所属の政治家。ボリス・ジョンソン (1964-) 政権下で 2022 年 7 月から 9 月まで、リシ・スナク (1980-) 政権下で同年 10 月から 2023 年現在まで保健相を務めている　ℓ44 **the Health and Social Care Secretary**「保健相」保健省 (the Department of Health and Social Care) の担当大臣。保健省はイギリスの政府機関で、イングランドの保健と社会保障に関する政策や NHS の監督などを担当している　ℓ46 **the (NHS) Pay Review Body**「(NHS) 給与審議会」イギリスの政府外公共機関。政府に対し、NHS の職員の賃金に関する助言を行っている。1983 年設立

イギリスの「ナース」

フローレンス・ナイチンゲール（Florence Nightingale, 1820-1910）は、イタリア生まれのイギリスの看護師で、近代看護法の創始者です。クリミア戦争の野戦病院で衛生状態の酷さに心を痛め、近代的病院の改革と職業看護師の育成に力を尽くしました。現代では「ナース」といえば職業看護師を思い浮かべますが、ナイチンゲール以前は少しニュアンスが違いました。もともとナースは「乳母」を意味しており、愛着を込めたナニー（nanny）という呼び方は今も使われています。英文学に登場する有名なナースの筆頭は、ウィリアム・シェイクスピア（William Shakespeare, 1564-1616）の『ロミオとジュリエット』（*Romeo and Juliet*, c. 1594）に登場するジュリエットの乳母です。また、オーストラリア生まれのイギリスの児童文学作家 P・L・トラヴァース（P. L. Travers, 1906-96）の『メアリー・ポピンズ』（*Mary Poppins*, 1934）に登場する魔法が使える辛口の乳母も、根強い人気を保っています。

MOVING ON

Making a Summary

CD 1-19

Fill the gaps to complete the summary.

The Royal College of Nursing have organised national strike action over pay and conditions, and this is the biggest (**w**⎵⎵⎵⎵⎵⎵⎵⎵) in London so far. They are asking for a pay increase of inflation plus 5%, but so far there have been no (**n**⎵⎵⎵⎵⎵⎵⎵⎵), despite the RCN saying they'd be prepared to meet the government half-way. They'll put any offer to the membership, but so far, all the government has said is that trade unions should (**e**⎵⎵⎵⎵⎵⎵⎵⎵) in a (**c**⎵⎵⎵⎵⎵⎵⎵⎵) dialogue about the Pay Review Body process for the coming year. Unions used to be against striking, but today, nurses are leaving in their (**d**⎵⎵⎵⎵⎵⎵⎵⎵) due to low pay. Members worry about safety, so they feel they should speak up and (**a**⎵⎵⎵⎵⎵⎵⎵⎵) for their patients. There has been some (**d**⎵⎵⎵⎵⎵⎵⎵⎵) to patients, but people should still go to hospital for urgent care. The (**d**⎵⎵⎵⎵⎵⎵⎵⎵) will not be over soon.

Follow Up

Discuss, write or present.

1. Perhaps you thought that nurses shouldn't be allowed to strike. Now we have heard that many nurses are leaving the profession because of low pay. In fact, their pay is falling. What do you think now? Should strikes be allowed?

2. Make a list of ten different jobs, and then consider how much a person doing that job should earn. Who should earn the most? Who deserves the least? Why?

3. Do some research and find out what has happened with the nurses' strike. Doctors have also been striking, along with teachers and other professions. Has this ever happened in Japan?

Unit 7

Sustainable Antarctic Cruises

南極にクルーズ船が到着しましたが、その目的は観光だけではないようです。科学者たちが大いに期待を寄せる新たな観光プロジェクトについて、ニュースを見てみましょう。

On Air Date   2 April 2022

STARTING OFF

Setting the Scene

What do you think?

1. If you had enough money for a sightseeing trip anywhere in the world for three weeks, where would you go, and why?

2. Some people think that tourism is bad for the world, and we should stay at home instead. Do you agree?

3. Have you ever taken a cruise on a ship? If you have, what was it like? If not, what do you think it would be like?

Building Language

Which word (1-8) best fits which explanation (a-h) ?

1. fragile   [   ]
2. sustainable [   ]
3. alluring   [   ]
4. remote   [   ]
5. impressive [   ]
6. monitor   [   ]
7. integrate   [   ]
8. logistics   [   ]

a. watch and check
b. very attractive or tempting
c. detailed planning and organisation of a large operation
d. easily damaged or destroyed
e. able to continue without using too many resources
f. a long way away; isolated
g. join or bring together
h. arousing admiration or respect

Understanding Check 1

Read the quotes, then watch the news and match them to the right people.

    a. Coming to places like Antarctica costs a lot …

    b. This presents its own unique challenges …

    c. This ship may be effectively used for, er, real science …

    d. … could tourism actually be part of the solution?

( )   ( )   ( )   ( )

Understanding Check 2

Which is the best answer?

1. The *Roald Amundsen* has many new features. Which one of the following was <u>not</u> mentioned.

    a. She is made of plastic that can be recycled.

    b. She has battery hybrid powered engines.

    c. She has equipment to analyse seawater.

    d. There is a scientific centre on board.

2. Which one of the following sentences best describes Professor Alia Khan?

    a. She has to spend five years in Antarctica sampling the snow.

    b. She collects data with the ship's facilities, and shows passengers what she does.

    c. She has a research grant to study ecological tourism.

    d. She always spends her vacations taking trips in the Antarctic.

3. How was the ship able to help the scientists on Livingston Island?

    a. The ship's doctor saved the lives of some of them.

    b. The ship became a temporary home for them.

    c. The ship provided transport when the supply ship was delayed.

    d. The ship supplied them with more food.

What do you remember?

4. Why are scientists in Antarctica worried about cruise ships? How have the newer ships changed?

_____

5. What is special about the crew on the *Roald Amundsen*?

_____

6. What does the scientific community hope the passengers will do when they return home?

_____

Background Information

　1820 年に南極大陸が発見されると、19 世紀には様々な国の探検家によって南極の科学的・地理学的探検が盛んに行われるようになりました。南極点への到達は、探検家ロアール・アムンセン (Roald Amundsen, 1872-1928) が率いるノルウェーの探検隊と、南極探検家のロバート・スコット (Robert Scott, 1868-1912) が率いるイギリスの探検隊が競っていましたが、1911 年 12 月 24 日にアムンセンが世界で初めて達成しました。一方、スコットも 1912 年 1 月 18 日に南極点に到達したものの、帰路で遭難し死亡しました。その後 1930 年代から 40 年代にかけて、世界各国が南極の領有権を主張し始めた結果、1959 年にイギリスや日本を含めた 12 ヶ国で南極条約 (The Antarctic Treaty) を締結し、南極の平和的利用、科学調査の自由と国際協力、核爆発や放射性廃棄物の処分の禁止、そして南極の領有権凍結等を決定しました。

　南極旅行については、1960 年代にアルゼンチン南端のウシュアイア (Ushuaia) から出発するクルーズ船での旅行が本格的に開始されて以来、様々な会社が船を運航しています。コロナウイルス流行前の 2019 年から 2020 年にかけて約 74,000 人が南極に足を運びました。南極を訪れるには、南極条約締結国が発行する許可書を取得する必要があります。また、クルーズ船は大量の石油燃料を積んで環境に影響を与えているとされており、その航行を抑制しようとする動きもあります。安全で環境に配慮した南極旅行を行うため、1991 年に設立された国際南極旅行業協会 (IAATO: The International Association of Antarctica Tour Operators) は、100 人以上の乗客を一度に同じ場所に上陸させてはならず、乗客が 500 人以上の船は乗客を 1 人も上陸させてはいけないという制限を設けています。

　環境に配慮した南極旅行が求められる中、ノルウェーのフッティルーテン (Hurtigruten) 社によって運行されている 2019 年製造のロアール・アムンセン号 (MS *Roald Amundsen*) は、全長 140 メートル、全幅 23.6 メートル、キャビン数 165 室の大型客船でありながらも燃料と電気のハイブリッドエンジンを持ち、電気エンジンだけでも約 30 分の運航が可能です。また、燃料消費も抑制し、二酸化炭素排出量を 20% 削減するなど、環境に優しい客船となっています。さらに、船内にはサイエンスセンターが設けられ、科学者が同乗して研究や講義などを行っています。環境に配慮した運行を行うだけでなく、乗客自身が自然、環境問題、野生生物、探検の歴史などについてプログラムを通して学ぶことのできる機会を提供しています。

参考:
https://www.rmg.co.uk/stories/topics/history-antarctic-explorers
https://www.hurtigruten.com/en-us/expeditions/ships/roald-amundsen/
https://iaato.org/

Filling Gaps

Watch the news, then fill the gaps in the text.

Newsreader: In Antarctica, scientists are concerned about the growing number of tourist cruise ships that could be damaging its (¹   ) ecosystem. But many of the newer ships are more (²   ), and even help to gather scientific data. So rather than being a problem, could tourism actually
5   be part of the solution? Julie Ritson reports.

Julie Ritson: 'Trip of a lifetime' is how many describe going to Antarctica. This incredibly (³   ) but (⁴   ) location attracts around 60,000 visitors each year. These tourists are travelling on the *Roald Amundsen*, an expedition cruise ship that uses battery hybrid powered engines, has an
10   (⁵   ) science centre, and equipment below deck that automatically analyses the surrounding seawater.

Ritson: This scientist, visiting the ship for the first time, wonders if it's (⁶   ) of doing even more.

Alexander Koloskov, senior scientist, Vernadsky Research Base: This ship
15   may be effectively used for, er, real science, not only for education, not only to spread information between the tourists, but the tourists can help to the science.

Ritson: Professor Alia Khan has a five-year research (⁷   ) from the US
20   National Science Foundation to study snow algae and how it (⁸   ) the rate that snow melts. But she can't spend five years (⁹   ) in
25   Antarctica, so joining a trip like this works well for her.

Professor Alia Khan, Western Washington University: I'm able to (¹⁰   ) some samples and data for my research, and I can use some of the (¹¹   ) on the ship, such as the microscopes, to look at the samples and then also work with the tourists to show them what I am sampling in the snow.

30   **Ritson:** Most of the ship's expedition crew also have science (¹²   ) and help run citizen science projects for the passengers.

Zoe Walker, science coordinator, Hurtigruten Expeditions: ... we have a little bubble of water on top and no air.

Ritson: Studying the microscopic phytoplankton in the water helps (¹³   ) the effects of global warming. Samples are (¹⁴   ) up and sent off to be analysed by researchers who can't get here themselves.

Walker: Coming to places like Antarctica costs a lot and takes a lot of planning. So by (¹⁵   ) citizens into their science, they are able to collect data (¹⁶   ) at the same locations throughout the season while the tourist ships are already here.

Ritson: Scientists also live and work in Antarctica for many months of the year. This presents its own unique challenges, (¹⁷   ) being one of them.

Ritson: This research base on Livingston Island is (¹⁸   ) home to around 40 scientists, but their supply ship has been (¹⁹   ), and they are running low on food. Luckily, our ship was nearby and able to help.

Ritson: For them, it's been a lifesaver that tourist ships cruise these waters.

Ritson: But what the scientific community really hope is that the passengers return home as (²⁰   ) who can educate others and help change behaviours that threaten this (²¹   ) environment. Julie Ritson, BBC News in Antarctica.

Notes

ℓ 8 the ***Roald Amundsen*** 「ロアール・アムンセン号」ノルウェーの海運会社フッティルーテンが 2019 年に造船した大型の探検船。ロアール・アムンセン（1872 年-1928 年）は 1911 年に人類で初めて南極点に到達したノルウェーの探検家の名前　*ℓ* 14 **Vernadsky Research Base** 「ベルナツキー基地」ウクライナの南極観測基地。1947 年に設置されたイギリスのファラデー基地（Faraday Station）を前身とし、1996 年にウクライナによって引き継がれた　*ℓ* 20 **National Science Foundation** 「国立科学財団」科学や工学の振興のために 1950 年に設立されたアメリカの連邦政府関係機関　*ℓ* 21 **snow algae** 「氷雪藻」高山や南極圏・北極圏に見られる、雪や氷上に生育する藻類　*ℓ* 26 **Western Washington University** 「ウエスタン・ワシントン大学」アメリカのワシントン州にある公立大学。1893 年創立のニュー・ワットコム教員養成学校（New Whatcom Normal School）を前身とする　*ℓ* 31 **citizen science** 「市民科学」科学の専門家ではない一般の人々がデータの収集やモニタリングなどを通じて参加することで行われる科学研究のこと　*ℓ* 32 **Hurtigruten Expeditions** 「フッティルーテン・エクスペディションズ」フッティルーテン・グループの旅行会社　*ℓ* 35 **phytoplankton** 「植物プランクトン」　*ℓ* 47 **Livingston Island** 「リヴィングストン島」1819 年に発見された南極海の島。南緯 60 度以南において発見された初めての島として知られる

南極大陸横断国際犬ぞり隊

　1989 年 7 月、アメリカ、フランス、ソ連、中国、イギリス、日本からの 6 人の冒険家や科学者で構成された南極大陸横断国際犬ぞり隊が、南極半島の先端のシール・ヌナタックを出発し、1990 年 3 月、ゴール地点であるミールヌイ基地に無事到着しました。南極大陸最長横断ルートへの挑戦で、220 日をかけて約 6,000 km を走破しました。しかし、翌 1991 年に「環境保護に関する南極条約議定書 (Protocol on Environmental Protection to the Antarctic Treaty)」が採択されたことで南極外からの生き物の持ち込みが禁止され、南極大陸内での犬ぞりの使用ができなくなりました。また、この隊が通過した南極半島のラーセン棚氷 (Larsen Ice Shelf) は、現在では大部分が 300 km にわたって崩落・消失しており、犬ぞりを使っての最長横断ルートの走破は、この 1 回限りとなってしまいました。

MOVING ON

Making a Summary

 CD 1-22

Fill the gaps to complete the summary.

　Antarctica is (r _____), but it is also very (a _____), and each year, it is visited by 60,000 people. Scientists are worried that all the cruise ships are damaging its (f _____) ecosystem. However, many newer ships are more (s _____). The *Roald Amundsen* has an (i _____) science centre, and the crew runs science projects for the passengers, who are often (i _____) into scientific research. One Professor, Alia Khan, helps students study how algae affects melting snow. Although her research grant is for five years, she cannot stay in Antarctica for that time, so joining the cruise works for her. Other researchers can stay at home, while their samples are collected and sent to them for analysis. For example, the passengers help (m _____) the effects of global warming by taking samples of (m _____) phytoplankton. Tourist ships can also help with (l _____) by supplying food to research bases when needed. It is hoped that when the passengers return home, they will educate others about Antarctica.

Follow Up

Discuss, write or present.

1. How would you feel about joining a cruise on the *Roald Amundsen*, and why?

2. At home, the passengers will help to change behaviour that threatens the environment. How do you think behaviour has to change?

3. If you were given a five-year grant to do research into anything you like, what would you study? (It doesn't have to be scientific.) And why?

Unit 8

The Wheelchair Rugby League World Cup

イングランドで 2022 年、新型コロナウイルスの影響で延期になっていたラグビーリーグのワールドカップが開催されました。今回のワールドカップにはこれまでとは異なる点がありましたが、一体どのようなものだったのでしょうか。

On Air Date   31 August 2022

STARTING OFF

Setting the Scene

What do you think?

1. What sports do you play, and what sports do you most enjoy watching? And why?

2. What do you think are the most physical and violent sports?

3. If you were unable to walk and needed a wheelchair, would you still want to play sports? What sports would you play?

Building Language

Which word or phrase (1-8) best fits which explanation (a-h)?

1. inclusive   [   ]
2. fainthearted   [   ]
3. vouch for   [   ]
4. brutal   [   ]
5. handle   [   ]
6. part and parcel [   ]
7. biased   [   ]
8. blown away   [   ]

a. lacking courage; cowardly; reluctant to take risks
b. invites and allows everyone, and all groups of people, to participate
c. cruel; vicious; savage; inhuman
d. give a personal assurance, promise, or guarantee about something
e. an essential and basic element of something
f. prejudiced; not completely fair or impartial
g. extremely surprised; shocked
h. manage, deal with, or be responsible for something that might be a bit tricky

WATCHING THE NEWS

Understanding Check 1

Read the quotes, then watch the news and match them to the right people.

a. … it's going to be looking at all these seats around now, you know …

b. So, it's going to be tight. Like it's going to be really tight.

c. We're all looking forward to it and, and, and ready to go.

d. Many of the wheelchair matches will take place at the Olympic Park.

( )   ( )   ( )   ( )

Understanding Check 2

Which is the best answer?

1. According to the news, which of the following statements is definitely correct?
   a. The first Wheelchair World Cup was held in 2022.
   b. The Wheelchair World Cup hasn't been held since the London 2012 Olympics.
   c. There's been a Wheelchair World Cup each year since the 2012 Paralympics.
   d. In 2022, the Men's, Women's, and Wheelchair World Cups were played alongside each other for the first time.

2. What does Jodie (the first woman) think of the brutality in the sport?
   a. She thought it was part and parcel of the sport, but now it is too much.
   b. She doesn't enjoy it and finds it hard to handle.
   c. She didn't enjoy it at first, but later expected to be hit, and gave hits too.
   d. She never found it brutal at all.

3. What does Tom, the English captain, think of England's chances?
   a. England have been working really hard, so he thinks they are going to win.
   b. He's biased and hopes they'll win, but they probably won't, as France are champions.
   c. As long as England don't play as badly as in June, they'll probably win.
   d. England are world champions, but France train hard, so it'll be close.

What do you remember?

4. Where are the Rugby League World Cup matches going to be played?

_____

5. What does Lewis King think the atmosphere at the games is going to be like?

_____

6. Does Adam Hills think that England are better than Australia? Who does he think will win when they play each other?

_____

Background Information

　ラグビーには大まかにラグビーユニオンとラグビーリーグの2種類があり、選手数や1トライの得点数などの違いがあります。ラグビーユニオンの方が世界的に人気で、日本でよく知られているラグビーもラグビーユニオンを指しますが、今回のニュースではラグビーリーグが扱われています。

　男子のラグビーリーグ・ワールドカップは、1954年にイギリス、フランス、オーストラリア、ニュージーランドの4チームで行われたのが始まりで、今回のイングランド大会で16回目になります。本来、2021年に開催される予定でしたが、新型コロナウイルスの影響で2022年10および11月に延期されました。16チームが参加した今回はオーストラリアが優勝しています。女子のラグビーリーグ・ワールドカップは2000年にイギリス、オーストラリア、ニュージーランドの3チームの参加で始まり、6回目となる今大会は8チームが参加し、オーストラリアが優勝しました。また、車いすラグビーリーグ・ワールドカップは2008年に4チームの参加により開始され、8チームが参加した今大会ではイングランドが優勝しました。

　車いすラグビーリーグは障がい者だけでなく、障がいのない人も男女関係なく参加することができるため、最も「インクルーシブ（包括的）」な競技だと言われています。さらに、今回のイングランド大会は、インクルーシブであることを大会の目標として掲げました。もともと男子、女子、車いす大会は別々に行われていましたが、今大会では初めて3つの種目が同時開催され、全試合がBBCで放映されただけでなく、出場国が得られる参加費や賞金も、男子、女子、車いすの全種目において同額が与えられました。政府のデジタル・文化・メディア・スポーツ省（DCMS: Department for Digital, Culture, Media, Sport）下の機関であるスポーツ・イングランド（Sport England）が約2,300万ポンド（約41億4,000万円）の資金援助を行い、そのうち約33万ポンド（約5,900万円）が世界初となるボランティア・プログラムに割り当てられました。そのプログラムでは、普段はケアを受けている側である障がいを持つ人々が、大会において主体的にボランティアを行いました。障がい者が積極的に役割を果たすことは、彼らの社会における新たな可能性の発見につながるだけでなく、人々にインクルーシブな社会に向けての意識改革を促します。今回のラグビーリーグ・ワールドカップは、競技の面白さだけでなく、包括性を人々に印象づけました。次回2025年にフランスで開催されるワールドカップにも期待が高まります。

参考：
https://www.rlwc2021.com/
https://www.sportengland.org/news/most-inclusive-rugby-league-world-cup-ever-set-kick
https://www.rlwc2021.com/social-impact/inclusion

Filling Gaps

Watch the news, then fill the gaps in the text.

Newsreader: Next, ten years on from holding the London 2012 Paralympics, this
autumn, the capital will help play host to what's been hailed as the most
(¹   ) World Cup of all time. For the first time, the Rugby League
World Cup consists of men's, women's, and wheelchair (²   ).

5   Many of the wheelchair matches will take place at the Olympic Park. Chris Slegg
has been to meet some of the players.

Chris Slegg: Wheelchair rugby league is not for the (³   ). Wales
international Jodie Boyd-Ward can (⁴   ) (⁵   ) that.

Slegg: From what I've seen of this sport, it's (⁶   ), it's so physical, but

10   you clearly enjoy that.

Jodie Boyd-Ward, Wales: Yeah. I mean, I didn't to begin with when I first started
all those years ago, er, I wasn't sure how to (⁷   ) that. But it's just
(⁸   ) (⁹   ) (¹⁰   ) of the sport, you know,
if you're going to play a contact sport, you expect to be hit. And also, you give

15   the hits too.

Slegg: England host the Rugby League World Cup this autumn. For the very first
time, the Men's Rugby League World Cup, Women's Rugby League World Cup,
and Wheelchair Rugby League World Cup will all take place (¹¹   )
each other.

20 **Slegg:** Well, nearly all of the matches in the Rugby League World Cup are taking
place in the north of England, but there are chances for Londoners to
(¹²   ) (¹³   ). One of the men's semifinals is at the
Emirates Stadium. And every match in Group A of the wheelchair competition,
that's England's group, takes place here at the Copper Box.

25 **Slegg:** Lewis from Dartford took up the sport when a blood clot left him
(¹⁴   ) to walk. He's now hoping to make the England squad, and
his first World Cup.

Slegg: What do you think the (¹⁵   ) is going to be like inside the
Copper Box?

30 **Lewis King, England:** Well, it's going to be looking at all these seats around now,
you know, if, if we can fill it up, it's going to be huge and probably the biggest
(¹⁶   ) that I would have played in front of. So, er, it's exciting and
it fills you full of emotions just being here now, looking around, and, probably,

46

the same emotions that we'll feel as players on the day when we come and play it.

Man: If you just turn your wrist slightly in …

Adam Hills, Rugby League World Cup ambassador: Okay.

Man: … that way the ball will then have a better trajectory going up.

Hills: Yeah, yeah. Okay.

Slegg: Trying out the sport for the first time, Australian comedian, a huge rugby league fan, Adam Hills.

Hills: I think I've found my new calling.

Slegg: Oh, I've spoken to an, an English player, a Welsh player, and an Irish player, because I wanted to be (**17**   ).

Hills: Yeah.

Slegg: They've all said England are better than Australia. Do you, do you accept that?

Hills: I, I would say that's possibly (**18**   ). You've got to remember whenever Australia play England in any sport, they lift about 25%. So, Australia might be this level and England at this level, but we'll get up there. So, it's going to be tight. Like it's going to be really tight. And I think for people who haven't seen wheelchair rugby league, they're going to be (**19**   ) (**20**   ) by what they see.

Slegg: Captain of the England team is Tom Halliwell.

Tom Halliwell, England Captain: I'm going to be (**21**   ) but I'd say I'm, so I'm going to say we, we're going to win it. Er, we've been working really hard and, and training really hard. And, er, we've, we've played a test match against France in June, and, er, we've won that against France, who were the current World Cup champions. So, yeah, it's quite (**22**   ). We're all looking forward to it and, and, and ready to go.

Slegg: The Wheelchair Rugby League World Cup begins at the Copper Box on November the 3rd. Chris Slegg, BBC London.

Notes

ℓ3 **the Rugby League World Cup**「ラグビーリーグ・ワールドカップ」ラグビーリーグの国際大会　ℓ5 **the Olympic Park**「オリンピック・パーク」2012年のロンドンオリンピック開催に向けてロンドン東部に建設された公園＜Unit 3参照＞　ℓ14 **contact sport**「コンタクトスポーツ」ラグビーリーグやラグビーユニオン、ボクシング、柔道など、選手同士の身体が接触するスポーツを指す　ℓ22 **the Emirates Stadium**「エミレーツ・スタジアム」ロンドンのイズリントン区ホロウェイにあるサッカースタジアム　ℓ24 **the Copper Box**「カッパー・ボックス」正式名称は「カッパー・ボックス・アリーナ (the Copper Box Arena)」で、オリンピック・パーク内に位置する　ℓ25 **Dartford**「ダートフォード」イングランド南東部のケント州にある地区　ℓ37 **Adam Hills**「アダム・ヒルズ（1970- ）」オーストラリア、シドニー南部の郊外にあるロフタス出身のコメディアン。先天的な右足の欠損により、義足を装着している

ラグビーの起源

Behind the Scenes

『トム・ブラウンの学校生活』(*Tom Brown's School Days*, 1857) は、イギリスの学校小説の先駆となった作品で、ウォリックシャーにあるパブリック・スクールのラグビー校 (Rugby School) を舞台に、文人マシュー・アーノルド (Matthew Arnold, 1822-88) の父、トマス・アーノルド (Thomas Arnold, 1795-1842) が校長だった時期の学校生活が描かれています。著者トマス・ヒューズ (Thomas Hughes, 1822-96) は卒業生で、主人公トム・ブラウンは、著者自身や、兄弟、友人の体験を元に造形されています。古典とスポーツを大事にして心身の成長を促すパブリック・スクールの教育が主題となっており、クリケット、長距離走と並んで、ラグビー・フットボールが登場します。その名の通り、ラグビー・フットボールは 1823 年にラグビー校で始まりました。ウィリアム・ウェッブ・エリス (William Webb Ellis, 1807-72) という生徒が、フットボールの競技中にボールを抱えて走り出し、それが新しい競技の原型となりました。

MOVING ON

Making a Summary

CD 1-25

Fill the gaps to complete the summary.

In autumn 2022, ten years after the London Paralympics, the Rugby League held the most
(**i**   ) World Cup of all time. The Men's, Women's and Wheelchair competitions
were all held alongside each other. One male player, Lewis King, said it was exciting and very
emotional to be there. It looks like a (**b**   ) sport, and Jodie, a female player, can
(**v**   ) for the fact that it is not for the (**f**   ). To begin with, she
wasn't sure how to (**h**   ) it, but then she realised it was (**p**   ) and
(**p**   ) of the sport. Adam Hills, a famous comedian, thought that people were
going to be (**b**   ) (**a**   ) by the sport. The game between England
and Australia would be very (**t**   ). Tom Halliwell, the Captain of England felt that
England would win because they had been training hard, and they had beaten the world
champions, France. However, of course, he was (**b**   ).

Follow Up

Discuss, write or present.

1. Watch some of the final on https://www.youtube.com/watch?v=8QPlNEACYBI
   Who won? Was it an exciting game? Do you think it was as brutal as people say?

2. One player in the video said that she expects to be hit, and enjoys hitting too.
   Why do you think wheelchair users would want to play a game like this?

3. Do a little research about the Paralympics. What other sports are included? Are
   any of them surprising? What do you think about them?

The First Female Mayor of Suginami

BBC ニュースで、杉並区初の女性区長の話題が取り上げられました。日本の女性政治家を取り巻く現状について、イギリスのニュースがどのように伝えているかを見てみましょう。

On Air Date   8 March 2023

STARTING OFF

 Setting the Scene

What do you think?

1. Do you vote in government elections? Why or why not?

2. How many women are there in Japanese national government, and how many women do you think there should be?

3. How do you think Japan compares to other countries regarding the representation of women?

Building Language

Which word or phrase (1-8) best fits which explanation (a-h)?

1. male-dominated [   ]
2. status quo [   ]
3. advocate [   ]
4. incumbent [   ]
5. diversity [   ]
6. representation [   ]
7. abysmal [   ]
8. inappropriate [   ]

a. the existing situation or state of affairs
b. controlled or governed by males
c. acting on behalf of a certain group of people in a decision process
d. unsuitable; not fitting; untimely
e. absolutely terrible; extremely awful
f. the state or quality of being different or varied
g. a person who speaks or writes in support of a cause or idea
h. a person who currently holds an office or role

WATCHING THE NEWS

Understanding Check 1

Read the quotes, then watch the news and match them to the right people.

   a. But those who do, have to deal with misogyny and harassment.

   b. … other women have told me about what they went through.

   c. … an opportunity to celebrate the achievements of women …

   d. As a woman, and especially fairly, fairly young, I am not from bureaucracy …

(   )   (   )   (   )   (   )

Understanding Check 2

Which is the best answer?

1. Which of the following sentences is <u>not</u> correct?

   a. Miss Kishimoto says that she is not a bureaucrat.

   b. Miss Kishimoto is the first of three mayors in the history of Suginami Ward.

   c. Miss Kishimoto used to live in Belgium.

   d. Miss Kishimoto thinks the underrepresentation of women is insane.

2. How did Satoko Kishimoto become mayor?

   a. In an election, she narrowly beat the incumbent.

   b. She was chosen by the Conservative Party.

   c. She stood for election, and won easily.

   d. The previous mayor resigned. The people wanted a woman to replace him.

3. Tomomi Higashi, a council member of Machida City, has been dealing with one issue in particular. What issue is that?

   a. the cost of living

   b. childcare

   c. women in education

   d. sexual harassment

What do you remember?

4. What is International Women's Day? Why is it particularly relevant to Japan?

_____

5. According to Khalil, why is it very difficult for women to pursue a political career, and what happens to those who do?

_____

6. Why has the government been criticised?

_____

Background Information

　世界経済フォーラム（World Economic Forum）によって毎年発表され、世界の男女間の不均衡を数値化しているジェンダー・ギャップ指数（Gender Gap Index）の 2022 年度版では、1 位はアイスランド、2 位はフィンランド、3 位はノルウェーで、イギリスは 27 位でしたが、日本は 146 ヶ国中 116 位で、主要 7 ヶ国（G7）で最下位となりました。「経済」「教育」「健康」「政治」の分野で指数が出されますが、日本は「教育」と「健康」については評価が高かった一方、「政治」における女性の進出については特に低く、146 ヶ国中 139 位となりました。2023 年 5 月時点での世界における国会議員の女性比率は、1 位がルワンダの 61.3%、2 位がキューバの 55.7%、3 位がニカラグアの 51.7%、イギリスは 48 位の 34.5% で、日本は 166 位の 10.0% でした。また、都道府県を含む全国の自治体においても女性首長はわずか 2% に留まっています。さらに、2023 年 1 月に共同通信が行った調査では、女性の政治家や指導者は性的嫌がらせなどのハラスメントを受ける可能性が男性よりも高いという結果が出るなど、女性の政治参加の難しさが浮き彫りとなりました。

　このような状況の中、2022 年 7 月、杉並区長に岸本聡子氏（1974-　　）が就任しました。岸本氏は学生時代に環境活動に参加し始め、国際青年環境 NGO の代表に就任後、オランダにある国際政策シンクタンクのトランスナショナル研究所（Transnational Institute）で研究員を務めていましたが、選挙の 2 ヶ月前に杉並区に移住し、当時の現職候補を 187 票差の接戦で破って杉並区初の女性区長となりました。彼女は環境先進都市、多様性のある社会の実現、ジェンダー平等などの政策を掲げるだけでなく、女性の政治進出の支援もしており、2023 年 4 月の杉並区議選で応援した 19 人の候補者のうち 15 人が女性でした。その結果、女性が過半数を占めるとともに、投票率も前回より 4.19% 上昇するなど、ジェンダー平等の実現が着実に進みつつあります。

　日本のジェンダー・ギャップ指数の低さに対し、政府も少しずつ対策を打ち出しています。2022 年 6 月に政府決定した「女性版骨太の方針 2022」では、「女性の経済的自立」や「女性の登用目標達成」等、指数が特に低かった経済と政治分野での目標を定めました。また、日本は 2022 年 5 月に世界経済フォーラムが主導する「ジェンダー平等加速プログラム（Closing the Gender Gap Accelerator）」への参加を決定し、さらにジェンダー平等に向けて動き始めています。これからジェンダー平等が実現されるのか、日本の今後が注目されています。

参考：
https://data.ipu.org/women-ranking?month=5&year=2023
https://www.weforum.org/reports/global-gender-gap-report-2022/
https://www.japantimes.co.jp/news/2022/08/18/national/politics-diplomacy/satoko-kishimoto-suginami/

Filling Gaps

Watch the news, then fill the gaps in the text.

Newsreader: Welcome back to BBC News. And this Wednesday, we mark International Women's Day, an opportunity to celebrate the achievements of women and also reflect on the (¹   ) challenge of gender equality. In the most recent Gender Gap Index Report (²   ) by the World

5   Economic Forum, Japan ranked 116th overall out of 146 countries. Our correspondent, Shaimaa Khalil, sat down with the first female mayor of one of Tokyo's biggest districts. She says challenging Japan's (³   ) politics is a difficult, but necessary job.

Shaimaa Khalil: This is not your (⁴   ) Japanese politician. Satoko

10 Kishimoto is an outsider, challenging the (⁵   ) (⁶   ). After living in Belgium for the last decade, Miss Kishimoto has become one of only three female mayors in Tokyo's 23 main districts, and the first in the history of the Suginami area. In June, the former environmental activist and democracy (⁷   ) beat the Conservative (⁸   ) by a

15 narrow margin. She tells me the first few months on the job have been a rough ride.

Satoko Kishimoto, Mayor of Suginami Ward, Tokyo: As a woman, and especially fairly, fairly young, I am not from bureaucracy,

20 bureaucrats, I'm not pro-, politician. So, then, automatically, you know, like, er, er, it's difficult. Issues like climate change, (⁹   ), you know, er,

25 the, the gender equality, of, er, er, of course, um, has been challenged by the kind of old politics or like, er, you know, the, the boys' club.

Khalil: In her own district, most of the senior political posts below that of mayor are (¹⁰   ) by men. With women making up just over 2% of Japan's

30 local leaders, being a female mayor is a (¹¹   ) job.

Kishimoto: The women's (¹²   ) have stayed almost the same from 75 years. This is quite insane. In Japan, what is the most difficult for women to, to challenge the political life is because they have to do a lot of care work. We have to recognise as a national crisis, you know, like this (^{13}) of women in politics.

Khalil: Japan is the world's third largest economy, yet it has an (^{14}) record when it comes to women in politics, ranking at the (^{15}) 10 of 146 countries. And yes, the traditional social norms here make it very difficult for women to (^{16}) a political career. But those who do, have to deal with misogyny and harassment.

Khalil: This group of researchers and female politicians is trying to change that. They're hoping that their confidential online consultations will (^{17}) more women to brave the world of politics.

Tomomi Higashi, council member of Machida City, Tokyo: Because I've been public about my experience with harassment, other women have told me about what they went through. I think almost everyone has experienced it. Being showered with insults by older men or being touched (^{18}), for example, it was a wake-up call for me.

Khalil: The government has been (^{19}) criticised for not doing enough to encourage more women to get into politics, with some arguing that the (^{20}) cabinet and ruling party are part of the problem. There are some (^{21}) success stories, but it will take generations for women to get equal seats at Japan's top decision-making table. Shaimaa Khalil, BBC News, Tokyo.

35

40

45

50

55

Notes

ℓ2 **International Women's Day** 「国際女性デー」1975 年、女性の権利の向上や社会進出を推進すべく、国連によって毎年 3 月 8 日に定められた記念日 ℓ4 **Gender Gap Index Report** 「ジェンダー・ギャップ指数レポート」世界経済フォーラムが 2006 年から発行している、世界各国におけるジェンダーの不平等を表す指標についてのレポート ℓ4 **the World Economic Forum** 「世界経済フォーラム」スイスのジュネーヴ州コロニー (Cologny) に拠点を置く国際的な非営利団体。世界的または地域的な経済問題に取り組むべく、経済・政治などの各分野の指導者同士の交流と連携を図っている。1971 年設立 ℓ9 **Satoko Kishimoto** 「岸本聡子 (1974-)」杉並区長。2022 年 7 月から現職 ℓ27 **the boys' club** 「ボーイズクラブ」男性中心の閉鎖的な派閥や人間関係のこと ℓ48 **Tomomi Higashi** 「東友美 (1984-)」立憲民主党所属の町田市議会議員。2018 年から現職

女性参政権運動の軌跡

　イギリスで全ての女性に参政権が認められたのは 1928 年ですが、その獲得までには壮絶な闘争がありました。サラ・ガヴロン（Sarah Gavron, 1970-　）監督による映画『未来を花束にして』（*Suffragette*, 2015）は、1912 年のロンドンを舞台に、女性参政権運動を克明に描き出しています。女性たちによる 50 年に及ぶ平和的な抗議が黙殺され続けた末、エメリン・パンクハースト（Emmeline Pankhurst, 1857-1928）は過激な抗争を呼びかけ、婦人社会政治同盟（WSPU: Women's Social and Political Union）を設立しました。娘のクリスタベル・パンクハースト（Christabel Pankhurst, 1880-1958）は、その活動を引き継ぎましたが、もうひとりの娘シルビア（Sylvia Pankhurst, 1882-1960）は、婦人参政権論者ではあるものの平和主義を奉じました。エメリンは繰り返し投獄されても抗争を諦めず、亡くなる数週間前、ついにイギリス政府は全ての女性に参政権を認める法案を可決しました。ちなみに世界で初めて女性の参政権が認められたのは1893 年のニュージーランドで、日本では第 2 次世界大戦後、日本国憲法が制定された 1946 年でした。

MOVING ON

Making a Summary

CD 2-04

Fill the gaps to complete the summary.

　Satoko Kishimoto is the first female mayor of Suginami Ward, having narrowly beaten the (**i**　　　　　　) in the 2022 election. She used to be an environmental activist and democracy (**a**　　　　　　), and now deals with issues like climate change and (**d**　　　　　　). Most senior political posts in Suginami are held by men, so it is a lonely job. Japan's politics is (**m**　　　　　　), but Kishimoto says that challenging the (**s**　　　　) (**q**　　　　　　) is a necessary job. Japan has an (**a**　　　　　　) record of women in politics, and she thinks it is insane that women's (**r**　　　　　　) has stayed the same for 75 years. She says it is difficult for Japanese women to change this because they have to do a lot of care work. Another reason is that they have to deal with (**m**　　　　　　), (**h**　　　　　　), and (**i**　　　　　　) touching. A group of researchers and politicians is hoping that online consultations will encourage women to be braver, but the government is not doing enough, so it will take generations for women to be treated equal.

Follow Up

Discuss, write or present.

1. Why do you think that so few women become involved in Japanese politics?

2. Do you agree with Satoko Kishimoto that the underrepresentation of women in government is a 'national crisis'?

3. What do you think can be done about the underrepresentation of women in Japanese government?

Unit 10

Rescue of an Ancient Tavern

イギリスでは古い建築物が大切に維持されていますが、長年愛されてきたパブが存続の危機に直面しています。中世の建築物を現代の安全基準に則って維持することはできるのでしょうか。

On Air Date   28 October 2022

STARTING OFF

Setting the Scene

What do you think?

1. Are you interested in old buildings?

2. Think of a building that you know about and consider 'old'. (It doesn't have to be famous.) Describe it, and talk about it with your partner.

3. If an old building is in bad condition, do you think it would be difficult to repair it? What might the biggest problems be?

Building Language

Which word (1-8) best fits which explanation (a-h)?

1. ruin   [   ]
2. obstacle   [   ]
3. scaffolding   [   ]
4. crumble   [   ]
5. knuckle   [   ]
6. posterity   [   ]
7. commission   [   ]
8. timber   [   ]

a. collapse into small pieces
b. wood used in the structure of a building
c. something that is in your way, preventing success
d. all future generations; all your descendants
e. a framework for holding workers and materials during construction or repair
f. state of being destroyed or severely damaged
g. give authority for some action; place an order for something to happen
h. the joint connecting a finger to the hand

WATCHING THE NEWS

Understanding Check 1

Read the quotes, then watch the news and match them to the right people.

    a. We've had the building inspected …

    b. A local enthusiast is attempting to rescue it …

    c. … if it's left in the current condition for much longer.

    d. … in order to repair spaces like this, to return them to their former glory …

( )   ( )   ( )   ( )

Understanding Check 2

Which is the best answer?

1. Which of the following is the most accurate description of the Cockpit Tavern?

    a. It was built half a mile from Eton in 1419.

    b. It was built 1,419 years ago in Eton High Street.

    c. It has been in Windsor Castle for more than 600 years.

    d. It was built in Eton High Street about 600 years ago.

2. Which of the Cockpit Tavern's possible features was <u>not</u> mentioned?

    a. a post for punishing offenders by whipping

    b. stocks for punishment

    c. a floor made of sheep's knuckle bones

    d. a well for water

3. How is the Council getting in the way of Roger Line?

    a. It does not recognise that Roger is an architectural expert.

    b. It says Roger must commission a survey, although he has completed one.

    c. It refuses to let Roger begin the work because he is not a historical expert.

    d. It says Roger's survey was not undertaken by a suitably experienced structural engineer.

What do you remember?

4. According to Ron Gower, what will happen if they don't start to repair the Tavern soon?

5. Can you remember some famous people who have stayed in the Cockpit Tavern?

6. What did the timber frame expert think?

Background Information

　ロンドンとイングランド南東部には、ヒストリック・イングランド（Historic England）が重要建造物第1級および第2*級に指定する建物が22,516件ありますが、その3.4%にあたる756件が2022年版「危機にある遺産（Heritage at Risk）」リストに登録されています。今回のニュースに出てきたコックピット（The Cockpit）もその1つであり、崩壊の危機に瀕しています。

　バークシャー州イートン（Eton）に立つこの建物の歴史は15世紀に遡ります。もとは中世の酒場（tavern）でしたが、17世紀には「アダムとイブ（Adam and Eve）」という名の酒場を兼ねた宿屋（inn）となり、地元の人々や著名な高官が数多く訪れました。また、建物の別棟は食肉処理場としても使われていました。「コックピット」という名前は骨董品店だった時代に名付けられ、定かではありませんが、かつてこの場所に闘鶏場（cockpit）があったことに由来しているという説があります。さらに、1930年代には喫茶店（tearoom）として名門イートン校（Eton College）の生徒や家族に親しまれるなど、長い歴史の中で様々な変遷をたどってきた建造物です。

　近年では1階部分を店舗とする居住用の建物として改修すべく工事が行われていました。しかし、2016年に開発業者が経営破綻したことで作業が中断されると、中途半端な状態で建物が放置されることとなり、急激に劣化が進んでいきました。2020年、地元議会はこの建物を早急に保護すべく通告を出しましたが、その結果、かえって複雑な法律の壁が立ちふさがり、その後の改修計画が難航する事態となりました。そのような状況下で、地元バークシャー州を拠点とする改修専門業者ストラクチュラル・リペアズ（Structural Repairs）が名乗りを上げ、約900万ポンド（約16億2,000万円）の費用をかけた新たな改修計画が始動することとなりました。長きにわたる歴史の中で増改築や修理が繰り返され、質の悪い建材が使われている箇所も多々あり、雨風にさらされて草木による浸食が進むなど、建物の劣化は深刻です。改修作業は困難を極めると予想されていますが、将来的にはもとの酒場として復活させ、中世風のゲストルームや土産物店を併設する観光名所として再び活気を取り戻すことが期待されています。

参考：
https://cockpiteton.co.uk/
https://historicengland.org.uk/images-books/publications/har-2022-registers/lon-se-har-register2022/
https://www.maidenhead-advertiser.co.uk/news/eton---eton-wick/178120/eton-s-oldest-building-to-undergo-9million-transformation.html

Filling Gaps

Watch the news, then fill the gaps in the text.

Newsreader: To a pub that was built more than six centuries ago, that's played host to kings and queens down the ages, and which now faces (¹   ). Less than half a mile from Windsor Castle, the Cockpit Tavern in Eton is on its last legs. A local enthusiast is attempting to rescue it,

5   but is coming up against, well, administrative (²   ). Luke Hanrahan reports.

Luke Hanrahan: Beneath the protective awning, underneath (³   ), a centuries-old building built in the Middle Ages. Known as The Cockpit, it's stood along Eton High Street since 1419. But this one-of-a-kind structure is

10   beginning to (⁴   ) to the ground.

Ron Gower, property expert: The (⁵   ) is that it will fall into such disrepair that it will be beyond saving, and I guess, we're now barely a year or so away from that point if it's left in the current condition for much longer.

Hanrahan: Roger Line is a

15   (⁶   ) expert who specialises in repairing old buildings.

Roger Line, structural expert: What we've got here, Luke, is one

20   of only a few of these floors in existence, and it's made up of sheep's (⁷   ) bones.

Hanrahan: He's desperate to rescue this (⁸   ) property …

Line: We've also got here is the village stocks. And over there, we've got the

25   whipping post from 1756.

Hanrahan: … preserving all its peculiar features for (⁹   ).

Line: The thing I life, love about this building is the fact, the age of it, and the history, the people who have visited it over the years. Apparently, it includes King Charles the Second, many of the prime ministers from Eton College, Ian

30   Fleming, who wrote James Bond. The list goes on and on and on, and my (¹⁰   ) is to save it and repair it, so the general public can visit it and enjoy it.

Hanrahan: This room is an incredible more than 600 years old and in order to repair spaces like this, to return them to their former glory, the (^{11}) is in the detail, down to the iron nails. This 602-year-old iron nail has had to be (^{12}) by hand.

Hanrahan: But Roger, who's worked alongside architectural and historical experts, says the Council is getting in his (^{13}). The Council, the Royal Borough of Windsor and Maidenhead, says the necessary consent to begin the work has not been granted, that Roger must (^{14}) a survey to be undertaken by a suitably experienced structural engineer and (^{15}) frame specialist.

Line: These are hand-drawn sketches of all the (^{16}) within the building.

Hanrahan: It's something Roger says he's already (^{17}).

Line: We've had the building inspected by the (^{18}) frame expert, which was recommended by Historic England, and it says to this end, I see no reason why the work should not (^{19}) on this building.

Hanrahan: An ongoing battle to save a unique building at the (^{20}) of this community. Luke Hanrahan, BBC London.

イギリスを彩るパブの看板

　　イギリスのパブには大きく鮮やかな看板が掲げられ、今日のイギリス的な風景を彩る要素の1つとなっています。もともと、中世イギリスにおいて酒を販売する店は、ツタやイチイなどの枝葉を束ねた棒を店先に突き出して目印にしていました。1393年、イングランド王リチャード2世（Richard II, 1367-1400）は、販売目的でエール（ビール）を醸造する者に対して看板の掲示を命じました。本来はエールの質を判断する検査官が酒を提供する店を容易に認識できるようにするのが目的でした。しかし、当時は識字率が低かったため、文字の読めない客でも店を判別できるように、店はこぞって看板に絵を用いるようになり、派手で人目を引く看板が多く作られるようになりました。歴代の国王や英雄の名前、有名な戦争や著名人の名前を店名に冠した店も多く、それぞれの店が趣向を凝らした様々な看板を掲げています。

MOVING ON

Making a Summary

Fill the gaps to complete the summary.

　　The Cockpit Tavern is on its last legs, and faces (**r**   ). It was built about 600 years ago on Eton High Street, less than half a mile from Windsor Castle. It has a long history, and many famous people have stayed there, but now it is starting to (**c**   ), beneath (**s**   ) and a protective (**a**   ). It is feared that within a year, the building will be beyond saving if nothing is done. Roger Line, a structural expert, is desperate to rescue this (**e**   ) property, in which there is a floor made of sheep's (**k**   ), the village stocks, and a whipping post, and to preserve it for (**p**   ). However, he feels that he is coming up against administrative (**o**   ). The Council says consent has not been granted, and he must (**c**   ) a survey by an experienced structural engineer and (**t**   ) frame specialist. But Roger says he's already completed a survey, and sees no reason why work should not begin to save this (**u**   ) building.

Follow Up

Discuss, write or present.

1. Do you agree that it is important to save the Cockpit Tavern?

2. Some years ago, Tokyo Station was also on its last legs, and a lot of money was spent restoring it. Why did they do that, and do you think it was the right thing to do?

3. Do you think that all old things should be preserved for posterity? Not just buildings, but also vehicles, tools, furniture, clothes, etc?

Unit 11

A New Treatment for Alzheimer's

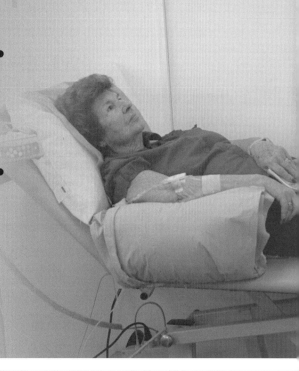

イギリスや日本を含む世界各国で、多くの人々が認知症を抱えながら生活しています。この度、認知症の一種であるアルツハイマー病の研究における画期的な成果が発表されました。一体どのような内容でしょうか。

On Air Date　30 November 2022

STARTING OFF

Setting the Scene

What do you think?

1. What do you know about Alzheimer's disease?

2. Do you know of anybody who is caring for a person with the disease? What sort of life do carers lead?

3. Do you know if there is any cure for Alzheimer's, or something that'll control the symptoms?

Building Language

For each word (1-8), find two synonyms (a-p).

1. herald   [　][　]
2. pivotal   [　][　]
3. clamour   [　][　]
4. relentless   [　][　]
5. underlying   [　][　]
6. impairment   [　][　]
7. bind   [　][　]
8. symptom   [　][　]

a. decisive	i. merciless
b. fundamental	j. demand
c. sign	k. announce
d. fasten	l. basic
e. agitation	m. indication
f. unstoppable	n. stick
g. introduce	o. damage
h. deterioration	p. climactic

WATCHING THE NEWS

Read the quotes, then watch the news and match them to the right people.

   a. This is so exciting because now we're getting results ...

   b. For the first time, scientists have found a drug that slows the onset of early-stage Alzheimer's disease.

   c. ... it appears to have had a very positive affect on Mavis.

   d. It can only help patients in the early stages of Alzheimer's ...

( )   ( )   ( )   ( )

Understanding Check 2

Which is the best answer?

1. What is lecanemab, the drug that they are talking about?
   a. It is a drug that can cure Alzheimer's disease.
   b. It is a drug that helps doctors to diagnose Alzheimer's disease.
   c. It is a drug that slows the symptoms of Alzheimer's disease.
   d. It is a drug that stops people from catching Alzheimer's disease.

2. Which one of the following sentences is correct about dementia in the UK?
   a. About 600,000 people in the UK are living with Alzheimer's.
   b. About a million people in the UK have Alzheimer's disease.
   c. About 400,000 people in the UK have dementia.
   d. Most people in the UK with dementia do not have Alzheimer's disease.

3. Which one of the following possible problems was <u>not</u> mentioned in the news?
   a. It doesn't help people who have had Alzheimer's for a long time.
   b. Some people in the trial had physical side effects.
   c. It will probably be very expensive.
   d. It changes the personality of the patients.

What do you remember?

4. How is this drug being described, and when will it be available?

_____

5. Can you explain what causes Alzheimer's and how lecanemab works?

_____

6. Why did Rodney and Mavis apply for the trial, and are they glad that they did?

_____

Background Information

　認知症には様々な原因がありますが、そのうちアルツハイマー病（Alzheimer's disease）が最も多く、約50%から70%を占めています。現在、世界で約5,500万人がアルツハイマー病を患い、2050年までには1億2,900万人を超えるとみられており、世界中でアルツハイマー病の治療に関する研究が行われています。アルツハイマー病は65歳前後で発症することが多く、物忘れから始まり、次第に複数の脳の機能に影響が及び、記憶障害、言語障害、人格の変化、幻覚や妄想などの症状に至る進行性の脳疾患です。根本的な原因はいまだ明らかになっていないものの、これまでの研究から、脳の神経細胞の外側に蓄積したアミロイドβタンパク質という有害なタンパク質の塊が神経細胞を減少させ、認知機能の低下をもたらすと考えられています。

　これまでの認知症の薬は、残された神経細胞の働きを促すもので、認知症の症状の進行を抑制することはできませんでした。しかし、今回ニュースで扱われている新薬レカネマブは、脳内のアミロイドβタンパク質を減らす作用があり、初期のアルツハイマー病の進行を抑制する画期的な薬として期待されています。レカネマブは日本のエーザイとアメリカのバイオジェン（Biogen）によって共同開発されました。2023年1月に医学誌『ニューイングランド・ジャーナル・オブ・メディシン』（*The New England Journal of Medicine*）において発表された研究によると、北米、ヨーロッパ、アジアの235施設で行われた治験の最終段階で、軽度のアルツハイマー病患者1,795人を対象に、レカネマブを投与するグループと偽薬を投与するグループに分けて検証が行われました。2週間に1度、18ヶ月にわたる投与の後、認知機能の変化を比較したところ、レカネマブを投与したグループは偽薬を与えられたグループより27%の割合で症状の悪化を抑制することができ、アミロイドβタンパク質の値もアルツハイマー病の水準を下回りました。

　2023年1月、レカネマブは米国食品医薬品局（FDA: US Food and Drug Administration）により迅速承認されました。日本でも厚生労働省の専門家部会が8月に承認を了承しました。イギリスでは医薬品・医療製品規制庁（MRA: Medicines and Healthcare products Regulatory Agency）に認可を申請中ですが、国民保健サービス（NHS: National Health Service）で薬が使用できるようになるには、国立医療技術評価機構（NICE: The National Institute for Health and Care Excellence）などの審査を受けなくてはならず、さらに数年がかかるのではないかと言われています。アルツハイマー病はどの国にとっても差し迫った課題であり、世界中がレカネマブに注目しています。

参考：
https://www.alzheimers.org.uk/
https://www.bbc.com/news/health-63749586

Filling Gaps

Watch the news, then fill the gaps in the text.

Newsreader: Now, let's move on to the day's other main story. For the first time, scientists have found a drug that slows the onset of early-stage Alzheimer's disease. It's been described as a (¹   ) breakthrough, following decades of failure in this field, and (²   ) a new era of possible
5   treatment for Alzheimer's, which is the most (³   ) form of dementia. Er, the medicine, er, is called lecanemab, and because the drug works in the early stages of the disease, many would, er, miss out unless early diagnosis and the rates for that are dramatically improved. Around a million people are thought to be living with, er, dementia in the UK. And Alzheimer's
10   affects around 60% of those, a disease which (⁴   ) destroys areas of the brain, affecting memory and understanding. And this new drug will not be available until it is officially (⁵   ), and it is likely to be an expensive treatment. Our medical editor, Fergus Walsh, has more details.

Fergus Walsh: Dementia is the most feared (⁶   ) among older people.
15   But Mavis Guinn, who's 88, is enjoying her retirement, such as coffee mornings, despite a diagnosis of early-stage Alzheimer's.

Mavis Guinn: I don't feel old. I don't feel tired, particularly. We enjoy life together. And I've got family, which I absolutely adore and enjoy them. Life, I think, is rather nice.

20   **Rodney Guinn:** Have you got tea?

Walsh: Mavis' short-term memory is badly affected, and she increasingly (⁷   ) on her husband, Rodney.

Rodney: What are you going to do with yourself today?

Mavis: I have no idea.

25   **Rodney:** Well, you're going up to have an infusion at the clinic.

Mavis: Oh, thank you. That, that's excited. Come on Rodney, let's get going.

Walsh: Mavis is one of nearly 2,000 patients who took part in a (⁸   ) trial of an experimental Alzheimer's treatment.

Dr Emer MacSweeney, CEO, Re:Cognition Health: So I'm just going to show
30   you the hippocampus, and that's where all our short-term memory is (⁹   ). And what you can see is that structure is very small and shrunken, and replaced by fluid because of the disease.

Walsh: Alzheimer's gradually destroys (¹⁰   ) areas of the brain involved in memory and understanding. The damage is driven by the buildup
35   of a rogue protein called amyloid, which clumps around neurons in the brain.

The new drug, lecanemab, (¹¹   ) to amyloid, which prompts
immune cells to attack and clear it from the brain. Access to the drug could be
severely limited, in part because specialist tests required to (¹²   )
patients for amyloid are not widely available. But there will be a
(¹³   ) for the treatment, which in the trial slowed cognitive decline   **40**
by about a quarter over 18 months.

Walsh: Lecanemab is not a cure. It can only help patients in the early stages of
Alzheimer's, but it is the first drug to convincingly slow cognitive decline. So
that makes it a breakthrough against this (¹⁴   ) disease.

Walsh: Doctors running the trial are delighted by the findings.   **45**

MacSweeney: This is so exciting because now we're getting results, the first
results that are indicating that the drug is successfully treating the
(¹⁵   ) cause and is slowing down the (¹⁶   ) of
cognitive (¹⁷   ) and also the behavioural (¹⁸   )
associated with Alzheimer's disease.   **50**

Mavis: You're nice and warm.

Walsh: Mavis may have been on a dummy or a placebo drug during the trial but is
now definitely getting lecanemab. She receives an infusion every two weeks at
this clinic in Surrey.

MacSweeney: No, I heard …   **55**

Mavis: Yes.

MacSweeney: … that you had a big coffee morning this morning.

Mavis: Oh, did I?

Walsh: Her Alzheimer's is still progressing. But her husband says it's not
(¹⁹   ) her of her personality.   **60**

Rodney: We don't want to just sit around and wait for the (²⁰   ),
which is why we, er, applied for the trial. And we're now extremely pleased that
we did so because, you know, it's, it, it appears to have had a very positive effect
on Mavis.

Walsh: Mavis had no (²¹   ) (²²   ) but others on the trial   **65**
did, including brain swelling and microbleeds. Lecanemab is far from being a
perfect drug. But Alzheimer's researchers say it points the way to better
treatments in future. Fergus Walsh, BBC News.

映画の中の認知症

1994 年、国際アルツハイマー病協会（ADI: Alzheimer's Disease International）は認知症への理解を推進するため、9 月 21 日を世界アルツハイマーデーに定めました。この病気に関する認識を高め、患者と家族に援助と希望をもたらすことを目的としています。

認知症患者や認知症と関わる人を描き、新たな気づきをもたらす小説や映画も多くあります。イギリス映画では、ハリー・マックイーン（Harry Macqueen, 1984-　）監督の『スーパーノヴァ』（Supernova, 2020）が力作です。コリン・ファース（Colin Firth, 1960-　）扮するピアニストのサムと、スタンリー・トゥッチ（Stanley Tucci, 1960-　）の演じる作家のタスカーは、ユーモアと文化を愛する長年にわたる同性の恋人同士ですが、タスカーが若年性認知症を患い、平和だった日常が蝕まれていきます。身近な人たちの体験から着想を得て、長期のリサーチを経て描かれた認知症の物語は、説得力をもって見る人の胸に迫ります。

MOVING ON

Making a Summary

 CD 2-10

Fill the gaps to complete the summary.

Alzheimer's disease is a (**r**　　　　　　　) disease which destroys areas of the brain involved in memory and understanding. It does this by building up a (**r**　　　　　) protein called amyloid. In Britain, about 600,000 people are living with it, and there is no cure. However, after a (**p**　　　　　　) trial, researchers have made a (**m**　　　　　　) breakthrough, which (**h**　　　　　　) a new era of possible treatment. A new drug, called lecanemab, works by (**b**　　　　　　) to the amyloid, which then prompts immune cells to attack it. By treating the (**u**　　　　　) cause, the drug can slow down the (**s**　　　　　) of cognitive (**i**　　　　　) associated with the disease. There is bound to be a (**c**　　　　　　) for the treatment. There are a number of problems to be solved: specialist tests are not widely available, it can only help patients in the early stages of the disease, and some patients had side effects. Lastly, it will be expensive.

Follow Up

Discuss, write or present.

1. In Setting the Scene, we discussed carers: people looking after Alzheimer's patients. How do you think they'd feel about this new drug?

2. The drug is going to be expensive. Why do you think it will be expensive? Should patients have to pay for it? What if they cannot afford it?

3. Care homes are expensive, and old people often spend all their savings. What do you think should be done about this situation? How does this compare to Japan?

Unit 12

Liverpool's Slavery Heritage

大英帝国の発展の裏側には、奴隷制の存在がありました。三角貿易の拠点の１つだったリヴァプールで、こうした歴史を見据えるための動きを見てみましょう。

On Air Date   5 April 2022

Eric Scott Lynch Slavery Histories

William Brown Street

Sir William Brown 1784 - 1864
Cotton Merchant, Banker, Philanthropist & Slave Owner

Liverpool's Central Library and World Museum have their origins in wealth accrued through slavery. William Brown became one of the main importers of slave-produced cotton into Liverpool. The Brown family also owned many enslaved people on their plantations in the United States. William Brown Street was named after him for funding these buildings.

DISCOVER MORE
liverpoolslaveryhistories.co.uk

STARTING OFF

Setting the Scene

What do you think?

1. What do you know about slavery?

2. When somebody mentions the city of Liverpool, what do you think of?

3. Do you think it is important for a city to remember its history?

Building Language

Which word or phrase (1-7) best fits which explanation (a-g)?

1. tip   [   ]
2. prosperity [   ]
3. repossess [   ]
4. resolution [   ]
5. integral   [   ]
6. flock   [   ]
7. fund   [   ]

a. being an essential part; necessary for something to be complete

b. help to pay for something

c. take back ownership of something, usually because it hasn't been paid for

d. success and wealth; a thriving condition

e. throw downwards; overturn; upset

f. a formal expression of a decision or intention, often after a vote

g. go to, or crowd around in large numbers

Understanding Check 1

Read the quotes, then watch the news and match them to the right people.

a. … there's long been a debate in this city about what to do about roads …

b. My father was a historian, but he was a historian with a purpose.

c. He became very wealthy through, um, trading cotton and also as a banker …

d. Now how does a city tackle the issue of its links with slavery?

( )   ( )   ( )   ( )

Understanding Check 2

Which is the best answer?

1. According to the news, which one of the following sentences is correct?
   a. Liverpool decided not to rename the streets named after slave merchants.
   b. Edward Colston was tipped into a Bristol dock two years before.
   c. Liverpool's streets were renamed because it wanted to face up to its history.
   d. Edward Colston has been tackling the issue of Liverpool's links with slavery.

2. According to the news, which one of the following sentences is <u>not</u> correct?
   a. Brown made a fortune by trading cotton and lending money to merchants.
   b. When Brown repossessed land, he returned it to the slaves working there.
   c. When the last plantation was sold in 1860, Brown gave £40,000 to Liverpool.
   d. Brown funded a museum and library, so a street was named after him.

3. How long has there been a black community in Liverpool?
   a. since 1860
   b. since the end of World War II
   c. There isn't a black community in Liverpool.
   d. for more than 300 years

What do you remember?

4. According to the news, what is one reason for Liverpool being so prosperous?

_____

5. How many plaques will be put up, and what is their purpose?

_____

6. Who was Eric Scott Lynch, and what did he want?

_____

Background Information

　17 世紀から 19 世紀におけるイギリス帝国の繁栄の一端を担ったのは奴隷制度でした。イギリスで製造した銃器などの工業製品をアフリカに運び、アフリカで得た黒人奴隷を西インド諸島や北米のプランテーションで労働させ、そこで生産した綿花や砂糖などをヨーロッパに持ち帰る三角貿易 (triangular trade) において、奴隷たちは大きな役割を担わされました。今回のニュースの舞台であるリヴァプールはこうした三角貿易の拠点として栄えた都市であり、奴隷や船乗り、留学のために来港したアフリカの君主の子息たちが定住したことで、イギリス最古と言われる黒人コミュニティが築かれた場所でもあります。

　黒人奴隷の子孫である歴史家エリック・スコット・リンチ (Eric Scott Lynch, 1932-2021) はリヴァプールと奴隷制との関わりを周知し語り継ぐべく活動した人物で、歴史を巡るツアーや国内外での講演、2007 年に実現した国際奴隷制博物館 (International Slavery Museum) の開館に向けてのキャンペーンなどを精力的に行いました。リンチの長年にわたる活動の結果、リヴァプール市議会は 2020 年 1 月、街の名士の名前を冠した通りなどに、その人物と奴隷貿易とのつながりなどを記したプラーク (plaque) を設置することを承認しました。そしてリンチの死後となる 2022 年、「エリック・スコット・リンチ奴隷制歴史プラーク (Eric Scott Lynch Slavery Histories Plaque)」として、最初の 1 枚となるウィリアム・ブラウン・ストリート (William Brown Street) のプラークを公開しました。

　これらの通りの名称自体の変更を求める声も以前から上がっていましたが、現在のところ実施には至っていません。しかし、2020 年にアメリカで始まったブラック・ライブズ・マター (BLM: Black Lives Matter) 運動がイギリスに波及したことで、人種差別撤廃を訴える動きが各地で白熱しているのは事実です。2020 年 6 月、リヴァプールと同じく奴隷貿易で栄えたブリストルで、黒人差別に反対する活動家らによって奴隷商人の像が引き倒される事件が起きました。また、リヴァプール大学 (The University of Liverpool) でも学生の抗議活動が起き、奴隷制廃止に反対したとされる元首相ウィリアム・グラッドストーン (William Gladstone, 1809-98) にちなんだ建物の名称を変更する意向が発表されました。差別を無くし、多様性を尊重しようとする流れの中、現在の価値観にそぐわない歴史的事実をどう受け止めるべきかが問われています。

参考：
https://www.liverpoolmuseums.org.uk/slavery-histories/eric-scott-lynch
https://www.bbc.com/news/uk-52954305

Watch the news, then fill the gaps in the text.

Newsreader: Now how does a city tackle the issue of its links with slavery? It's a question which has been debated ever since the statue of the slave trader, Edward Colston, was (^{1}) into a Bristol dock two years ago. Many of Liverpool's streets are named after (^{2}) who bought or sold

5   slaves, and there were calls for those streets to be renamed, but the city has decided it's better to keep the names and (^{3}) (^{4}) (^{5}) its history, as Phil McCann explains.

Phil McCann: William Brown, Liverpool cotton trader, Lancashire MP, slave owner. Today …

10 **Michelle Charters, Liverpool Slavery Streets Panel:** I would like to thank you all for coming along, to (^{6}) this important day in Liverpool's history.

McCann: One more step was taken on Liverpool's journey of coming to (^{7}) with the facts that its (^{8}) was thanks, in no small part, to slaves.

15 **McCann:** This street outside Liverpool's World Museum is named after William Brown, and this plaque tells people his full story. In a city which, it's often said, has the oldest established (^{9}) black community in the country.

Charters: We have had a (^{10}) since 1710, so

20   2022, to finally get offered this plaque is very important for us as a community.

McCann: This street is named after William Brown because he

25   (^{11}) the building of the museum, and the library next door.

Laurence Westgaph, founder, Liverpool Black History Research Group: He became very wealthy through, um, trading cotton and also as a banker, and he started to lend money to (^{12}) who owned plantations, and if he

30   ever had to foreclose on those loans, not only did he (^{13}) the land but also the human beings who worked on those plantations. They didn't sell the last of their plantations until 1860, and in that year, he gave £40,000 for the building of our beautiful, um, museum and library.

McCann: There are still lots of pretty recently written guides that (^{14}) William Brown but not his links to slavery, and there's long been a debate in this city about what to do about roads like this, and whether in fact they should be renamed. But two years ago now, the council passed a (^{15}) to erect plaques on this street and nine others.

Joanne Anderson, Mayor of Liverpool: Our fantastic buildings that we see are results of the (^{16}) that was made from slavery. So, to have all plaques, you know, inform people, and educate people about our past is really important.

McCann: These plaques are the result of years of campaigning by Eric Scott Lynch.

Andrew Lynch, Eric Lynch's son: My father was a historian, but he was a historian with a purpose.

McCann: Eric (^{17}) (^{18}) last year.

Lynch: He wanted the black people in Liverpool to be recognised for who they are: an (^{19}) part of the city.

McCann: Nine more streets will host plaques when owners and planning consents are sorted, but from now the thousands who (^{20}) here to see Liverpool's heritage will also see its true history. Phil McCann, *BBC Northwest Tonight*, Liverpool.

35

40

45

50

55

Notes

ℓ 3 **Edward Colston**「エドワード・コルストン（1636-1721）」イギリスの奴隷商人、慈善家。救貧院・慈善学校などの設立や慈善施設へ 70,000 ポンド以上もの寄付をした　ℓ 3 **Bristol**「ブリストル」イングランド南西部のエイヴォン川に臨む市。エイヴォン川河口に貿易港がある　ℓ 4 **Liverpool**「リヴァプール」イングランド北西部マージーサイド州の市。マージー川河口にあり、イギリス第 2 の海港をもつ　ℓ 8 **William Brown**「ウィリアム・ブラウン（1784-1864）」イギリスの商人、銀行家、慈善家　ℓ 8 **Lancashire**「ランカシャー」イングランド北西部の州　ℓ 15 **World Museum**「世界博物館」リヴァプール最古の博物館。1853 年開館　ℓ 16 **plaque**「プラーク」歴史的な出来事があった場所に設置される銘板　ℓ 48 **Eric Scott Lynch**「エリック・スコット・リンチ（1932-2021）」イギリスの地域歴史家、黒人人権活動家　ℓ 56 ***BBC Northwest Tonight***「BBC ノースウェスト・トゥナイト」BBC ノースウェストが夜に放送しているニュース番組

アメイジング・グレイス

世界で最もよく知られる讃美歌の1つ「アメイジング・グレイス」("Amazing Grace," 1772) はイギリスの牧師ジョン・ニュートン (John Newton, 1725-1807) によって作詞されました。彼は11歳で船乗りになり、35歳までアフリカから黒人奴隷を輸送する大西洋奴隷貿易 (Atlantic Slave Trade) に従事しました。その後神学を勉強して牧師となり、讃美歌を書き始めました。『オウルニィ讃美歌集』(*Olney Hymns*, 1779) 収録の「アメイジング・グレイス」では奴隷貿易に関わった自身の悔恨と許しを与えてくれた神の恩恵への感謝の念が歌われ、その頃から奴隷制廃止運動に関与し始めました。この讃美歌は19世紀にバプティスト (Baptist) とメソジスト (Methodist) の宣教師たちがアメリカ南部で宣教する際によく歌われ、黒人奴隷の間にも広まりました。現在もアメリカでは様々な場面で世俗の聴衆にも広く歌い継がれています。

MOVING ON

Making a Summary

 CD 2-13

Fill the gaps to complete the summary.

The (**p**   ) of British cities is largely thanks to slaves, and cities have been debating their links with slavery since a statue of Edward Colston was (**t**   ) into a Bristol dock. In Liverpool, the council passed a (**r**   ) to erect ten (**p**   ) on streets named after people who profited from slavery, explaining the links of each street with slavery. Liverpool's black community has been there since 1710, longer than in any other British city, and so has an (**i**   ) role in its history. William Brown Street is named after a famous person from Liverpool, who (**f**   ) the museum and the library with a gift of £40,000 in 1860. However, up to now, guides have not mentioned his links with slavery. In fact, he lent money to people who owned slaves, and when they couldn't repay, he (**r**   ) both the land and the slaves. Now, thousands who (**f**   ) to see Liverpool's heritage will also read about its true history.

Follow Up

Discuss, write or present.

1. What do you think of Liverpool's policy not to hide the city's links with slavery, but to be open and make sure people know about the city's true history?

2. What do you think of William Brown? Was he an evil person? Should his descendants pay compensation to the families of the slaves he owned?

3. In 1860, Brown gave £40,000 towards Liverpool's new museum and library. Today, that is equivalent to £6,200,000, or ¥1,116,000,000. If you had that amount to give away, what would you do with it, and why?

Unit 13

New Businesses in Sunderland

経済の伸び悩むイギリスで、町おこしに力を入れている地方都市があります。サンダーランドの取り組みはどのようなものなのでしょうか。ニュースを見てみましょう。

On Air Date   19 October 2022

STARTING OFF

Setting the Scene

What do you think?

1. Look at the map at the front of this book and find Sunderland. What country is it in (England, Wales, Scotland or Northern Ireland)? How far is Sunderland from London? What other city is it close to?

2. Make a list of all the types of small business that you know of.

3. What do you think small businesses need in order to start being successful?

Building Language

Which word or phrase (1-7) best fits which explanation (a-g)?

1. entrepreneur [   ]
2. struggle [   ]
3. posh [   ]
4. neglect [   ]
5. upmarket [   ]
6. immersive [   ]
7. niche [   ]

a. business owner who uses initiative to try to make profit by taking risks
b. provides information for a number of senses: sight, sound, touch, etc.
c. ignore; fail to give enough care or attention to something
d. expensive; designed for affluent customers rather than poor ones
e. a place or business position that is particularly suitable for somebody
f. upper class; perhaps snobbish
g. a fight or great effort to overcome a difficulty

WATCHING THE NEWS

Understanding Check 1

Read the quotes, then watch the news and match them to the right people.

  a. But now, it's back.

  b. Having the client base that I have now, like watching it grow …

  c. It's really busy, seven days a week, it's available throughout the year.

  d. … Sunderland has nonetheless become home to lots of new businesses …

( )   ( )   ( )   ( )

Understanding Check 2

Which is the best answer?

1. Which of the following descriptions of The Stack at Seaburn is <u>not</u> correct?
   a. Since its 2020 opening, The Stack at Seaburn has become a hub for businesses.
   b. All costs have gone up so much that there has been a drop-off in sales.
   c. They are worried about costs, but business is not bad.
   d. Sales haven't dropped although times have been difficult financially.

2. Which of the following descriptions of Mackie's Corner is most correct?
   a. When Watson lived in Sunderland, it was forgotten, but now it is back.
   b. Mackie's Corner was redeveloped recently, but people forgot about it.
   c. Mackie's Corner was neglected because it wasn't upmarket enough.
   d. It used to be posh, then it was neglected, but now it's upmarket again.

3. What did Andy Watson conclude after talking to these entrepreneurs?
   a. Experts think that bright times are ahead, but the businesses are uncertain.
   b. Despite the worries of experts, it seems that these businesses are going to succeed.
   c. Both experts and businesses are optimistic about the future.
   d. The businesses he visited agree with the experts that hard times are ahead.

What do you remember?

4. What two things are lots of new businesses in Sunderland benefiting from?

_____

5. Why does David (the 62-year-old) think better times are ahead?

_____

6. Watson was wearing a virtual reality headset, which was part of an immersive lab. According to Ashmita, why is this used with young people?

_____

Background Information

　イギリス北東部のタイン・アンド・ウィア（Tyne and Wear）州にあるシティ・オブ・サンダーランド（City of Sunderland）は、北海に面したウィア川（the River Wear）の河口周辺に広がる港湾都市サンダーランドを拠点とする人口約 27 万人の都市圏です。19 世紀から 20 世紀初頭にかけて、造船業やウィアマス炭鉱（Wearmouth Colliery）での採炭、サンダーランド発電所（Sunderland Power Station）の石炭火力発電事業などにより急速に発展しました。しかし、20 世紀半ばになると失速し、多くの造船所が閉鎖され、1976 年には発電所が廃止、1993 年には炭鉱が閉山されました。また、1806 年の創業以来地域の雇用を生み出してきたヴォー・ブルワリー（Vaux Brewery）の醸造所も 1999 年に閉鎖されました。

　伝統的な産業の衰退に伴い、サンダーランド市議会は長年にわたり地域再生に取り組んできました。1984 年には日産自動車の製造工場を誘致し、1992 年にはテクノロジーやサービス関連企業が集まるドックスフォード・インターナショナル・ビジネスパーク（Doxford International Business Park）を開設するなど、新たな産業を通じての地域活性化を進めています。今回のニュースに登場するサンダーランド・ソフトウェア・シティ（Sunderland Software City）は 2020 年に開館したサンダーランド・ソフトウェア・センター（Sunderland Software Centre）というビジネスセンター内にあり、テック企業等のビジネス支援やコンサルタントを行っています。

　市議会は現在、醸造所跡地を含む河岸周辺地域の再生に力を入れており、「リバーサイド・サンダーランド（Riverside Sunderland）」と呼ばれる大規模な再開発計画を 2020 年に本格的に発表しました。発表の前年には総合オフィスビルのザ・ビーム（The Beam）が完成し、2021 年には新市庁舎であるシティホール（City Hall）が開館しました。環境に配慮した住宅の建設も進められており、ビジネスや生活の拠点として発展していくことが期待されています。また、海辺のリゾート地の活性化も進められています。シーバーン（Seaburn）にあるスタック（The Stack）は臨海地域再生計画の一環として 2020 年に開館した総合レジャー施設で、レジャーや小売、ホスピタリティ業界等の起業家にとってのビジネスチャンスになると思われていましたが、昨今の物価上昇などの影響で撤退するテナントが相次いでおり、苦戦を強いられています。

参考：
https://www.sunderlandsoftwarecity.com/
https://www.riversidesunderland.com/
https://www.makeitsunderland.com/business-sites
https://www.bbc.com/news/uk-england-tyne-64596148

Filling Gaps

Watch the news, then fill the gaps in the text.

Newsreader: Now, despite the economic challenges of the past few
(¹) here in the northeast of England, Sunderland has
nonetheless become home to lots of new businesses benefiting from investment
in the city centre and the (²) redevelopment. Just over 1,500
5   new companies were set up here last year. Now the BBC Sunderland reporter,
Andy Watson, has been to meet some of the city's (³).

Andy Watson: For many people, Sunderland is an attractive place to live, and
importantly for the local economy, somewhere to start a business. The Stack at
Seaburn opened in 2020. It's become a hub for local businesses along the
10   (⁴), despite difficult financial times.

Neill Winch, Chief Executive, Danieli Holdings: All (⁵) have
gone up, certain utilities, packaging, foods, labour, so it is a concern. Er,
however, er, we're not seeing any drop-off in sales.

Mark Potts-Brown, Woofs N Scruffs: I just came up with the idea of, er, the
15   self-service baths walk-in service—you don't need an appointment—where
owners can come off the beach and bath and drive off with the dog. It's really
busy, seven days a week, it's available throughout the year. This season, we
have seen a (⁶) but we'll, we'll come through it.

Watson: Hi Laurie, are you all right?

20 **Laura Benson, Arch Brow Bar:** Hi,
yeah, yeah.

Watson: Just around the corner a
young (⁷) has
found her (⁸).

25 **Benson:** Having the client base that I
have now, like watching it grow
for the last year and a half, something I'm really proud of.

Watson: As someone who's been born and raised in Sunderland, I'd heard that
Mackie's Corner was the (⁹) end of the town. But in recent years,
30   it's been forgotten about and (¹⁰). But now it's back.

Watson: An (¹¹) gentleman's outfit has opened just last year. The
business is proud to be involved in the redevelopment of the city, something
that's not gone (¹²) by customers.

David Caslaw, customer: I mean, I'm 62 and this is the highest level of investment I've seen, probably since the late 1960s, and it's long (^13). So, er, I think better times ahead.

Watson: The city is also focusing on investing in the growth of the tech (^14). At Sunderland Software City, they've helped (^15) more than 100 new businesses since 2020.

Watson: I'm currently looking at a photo frame, and butterflies are flying out of the frame.

Watson: Augmented and virtual reality tech has been adapted by (^16) here.

Ashmita Randhawa, Head of Innovation, Sunderland Software City: We actually have a lot of young people come through our (^17) lab that, that we have, and, er, part of this kit that you're wearing is used with young people to excite them, inspire them about careers and, and pathways into STEM.

Watson: So although experts (^18) an uncertain future, the view from the businesses we visited is that bright times are ahead. Andy Watson, BBC News, Sunderland.

35

40

45

50

55

Notes

ℓ2 **Sunderland**「サンダーランド」イングランド北部タイン・アンド・ウィア州の港湾都市　ℓ8 **The Stack**「スタック」サンダーランドのシーバーン地区にある複合的レジャー施設。2020 年創業　ℓ9 **Seaburn**「シーバーン」サンダーランドの臨海部にある地域　ℓ11 **Danieli Holdings**「ダニエリ・ホールディングス」スタックを運営する企業。2008 年設立　ℓ29 **Mackie's Corner**「マッキーズ・コーナー」サンダーランド市街の中心部にある老舗のデパート。1840 年代にラルフ・ハッチンソンによって建てられ、帽子職人ロバート・マッキーの製造販売の人気で愛称を得たが、20 世紀末に荒廃した。2017 年、地元の不動産業と地域開発業を営むカートリー家により再建された　ℓ42 **Sunderland Software City**「サンダーランド・ソフトウェア・シティ」イングランド北東部のテクノロジー関連企業の支援を行う組織。2008 年設立　ℓ46 **augmented (reality)**「拡張現実」現実の風景に対し、コンピュータで情報を付加または合成して表示する技術　ℓ52 **STEM**「ステム」科学 (science)、技術 (technology)、工学 (engineering)、数学 (mathematics) の頭文字で、これらの科目の包括的な名称

サンダーランド・アソシエーション・フットボールクラブ（Sunderland Association Football Club）は1879 年に設立され、過去には 1 部のプレミアリーグ（Premier League）で 6 回の優勝経験がありながらも、近年は 2 部と 3 部に留まっています。しかし、地域の熱狂的サポーターによって愛されており、ホームスタジアムは入場者数の多さで知られています。2 部に降格した 2017-18 年シーズンを追ったドキュメンタリー『サンダーランドこそ我が人生』（*Sunderland 'Til I Die*, 2018）には 1 部復帰を目指すチーム関係者の苦悩や地域の熱狂的なファンの姿が映し出されています。労働者階級の街であり、造船業や炭鉱業といった産業が終了したサンダーランドの人々にとってサンダーランド AFC は唯一の娯楽であり救いとなっており、この作品では、地域と密接につながったチームの姿を見ることができます。

MOVING ON

Making a Summary

CD 2-16

Fill the gaps to complete the summary.

Sunderland has recently been investing in its city centre and coastal development, which has attracted (**e**   ), and 1,500 new companies. One example is The Stack at Seaburn, which has become a hub for local businesses despite a huge interest in costs. Another example is a new self-service baths walk-in service for dogs, whose owner thinks he will succeed, despite it being a (**s**   ). Another nearby example is a young (**e**   ) who has found her (**n**   ). Mackie's Corner used to be (**p**   ), but then became (**n**   ), until investment in redevelopment brought more (**u**   ) shops. One man said he saw better times ahead, as this was the most investment he had seen since the late 1960s. Finally, at Sunderland Software City, Sunderland is investing in the tech sector. One startup has an (**i**   ) lab, in which young people use (**a**   ) and (**v**   ) (**r**   ) headsets, which inspires them about careers in STEM. Businesses are optimistic about the future.

Follow Up

Discuss, write or present.

1. If you inherited ten million yen, and you had to build a business to earn a living, what kind of business would you choose, and why?

2. Watson talked about "the posh end of town". Do towns and cities in Japan have a 'posh' end? Where might they be?

3. A lot of young people at high schools are encouraged to study STEM. Why do you think this is, and do you agree with such a policy?

Unit 14

Brexit: How Do We Feel Now?

イギリスが EU から離脱して 3 年が経過しましたが、
一般市民は離脱後のイギリスについてどのように感じ
ているのでしょうか。ある町の人々の意見を聞いてみ
ましょう。

On Air Date   29 January 2023

STARTING OFF

Setting the Scene

What do you think?

1. What does 'Brexit' mean?
2. What is the European Union?
3. Do you know why the United Kingdom left the EU?

Building Language

For each word (1-7) find two synonyms (a-n).

1. gauge   [   ][   ]
2. alienate   [   ][   ]
3. dominate   [   ][   ]
4. turmoil   [   ][   ]
5. impact   [   ][   ]
6. unfold   [   ][   ]
7. unresolved   [   ][   ]

a. effect	h. separate
b. monopolise	i. incomplete
c. judge	j. divide
d. measure	k. chaos
e. evolve	l. dictate
f. undecided	m. significance
g. disturbance	n. develop

WATCHING THE NEWS

Understanding Check 1

Read the quotes, then watch the news and match them to the right people.

a. ... then I think the country would be in a totally different but better position.

b. I mean, it's just, there's just so many, so many things.

c. ... but no one wants to talk about it anymore.

d. ... but others have already changed their minds.

( )   ( )   ( )   ( )

Understanding Check 2

Which is the best answer?

1. Why have the BBC journalists been visiting Stratford-upon-Avon regularly?
   a. Although 48% of the country voted to leave the EU, Stratford voted to remain.
   b. It is three years since the UK left the EU, and Stratford has changed every year.
   c. It is the birthplace of Shakespeare, the local people know a lot about the UK.
   d. In Stratford, 52% voted to leave, which is the same as the nation as a whole.

2. What has happened since the UK left the EU?
   a. It appears that Brexit has been a great success.
   b. There has been turmoil, so we don't yet understand the impact of Brexit.
   c. Because of the COVID pandemic, Brexit has been an economic, social, and political failure.
   d. Brexit is still dominating politics, and people are still arguing about it.

3. In the news, we hear the opinions of four men and three women. Which one of the following is a correct description of their opinions?
   a. Nobody has changed their minds about Brexit.
   b. Although they were divided in the referendum, now everybody agrees.
   c. Some think Brexit was a mistake, but others think they should wait and see.
   d. Some people who voted to remain now wish they had voted to leave.

What do you remember?

4. Some of the people expressed their support for Brexit, for a number of reasons. Can you remember what they said?

_____

5. Some of the people think that Brexit was a bad idea, because it had brought a lot of problems. Can you remember what they said about Brexit?

_____

6. What was Richard (the last man to speak) unhappy about?

_____

Background Information

　イギリスは 2016 年 6 月 23 日に行われた国民投票で EU 離脱を決定し、2020 年のほぼ 1 年間の移行期間を経て、2020 年 12 月 31 日午後 11 時に EU を離脱し、EU 法が適用されなくなりました。それまで国内とほとんど変わらない手続きで行われていた EU 各国との輸出入に煩雑な手続きが必要となり、2021 年初頭には、傷みやすい食肉などを中心に、食品の輸出額が空前の最低値を記録しました。しかし、ちょうど同じ頃、新型コロナウイルスの感染が拡大し始め、世界的な大流行となりました。その結果、特に外食産業は大打撃を受け、世界中の国々で経済活動が停滞しました。さらに、2022 年 2 月にはロシアによるウクライナ侵攻が始まり、エネルギーや食料品の高騰が続きました。そのため、EU 離脱がイギリスの経済に実際にどのような影響を与えたのかを見極めることは大変難しくなっています。しかし、怒涛の 3 年を経て、EU 離脱のイギリス社会への影響を評価しようとする論調が広まっています。

　一般の人々の反応は様々です。国民投票で決定した以上後戻りはできないという見方が賛成派と反対派両方の主流ですが、賛成票を投じた人の中には、情報が不十分で判断を誤ってしまった、と振り返る人々もいます。また、様々な社会情勢のため世界中の国々の経済が打撃を受けましたが、イギリスは EU 離脱のためそれがより大きく、離脱していなければ少しは打撃を小さくすることができていた、と論じる人々もいます。さらに、イギリスの EU 離脱後の惨状を見て、EU に加盟する国々の中の離脱派が考えを改め、EU 内部を改革する方向へ論調を変えていったとする見方もあり、EU を離れたイギリスの行方に関心が高まっています。

　また、ニュースでも取り上げていたとおり、EU 離脱に賛成する人々の中でも政府の舵取りに不満の声が上がっています。現在、人々の関心が高まっている問題に、「権利章典（Bill of Rights）」があります。1998 年に「欧州人権条約（ECHR: European Convention on Human Rights）」に従ってイギリスで制定された現行の「人権法（Human Rights Act）」ではイギリスの主権が守られないという批判があり、ボリス・ジョンソン（Boris Johnson, 1964-　）の政権時に法案が提出されました。リズ・トラス（Liz Truss, 1975-　）政権下で一旦棚上げされましたが、リシ・スナク（Rishi Sunak, 1980-　）現首相のもと、再度検討されることになりました。しかし、権利章典では十分に人権が擁護されていないとして、廃案を求める声も上がっています。EU 離脱後の国の在り方は、議論が始まったばかりと言えそうです。

参考：

https://www.bbc.com/news/business-64450882

https://www.theguardian.com/commentisfree/2023/jan/13/european-brexit-britain-european-eu

https://www.bbc.com/news/newsbeat-32692758

Filling Gaps

Watch the news, then fill the gaps in the text.

Newsreader: This week marks three years since the UK's official departure from the EU in January 2020. Since then, we've regularly visited the town of Stratford-upon-Avon, where 52% voted 'leave' and 48% voted 'remain', (¹   ) the national result. As the third anniversary approaches, our
5   political correspondent, Alex Forsyth, returned this month to the town to (²   ) how people now feel about Brexit.

Chorus: Brexit.

Alex Forsyth: It was a day of celebration for some, sorrow for others. In Stratford-upon-Avon, pro-EU activists (³   ) to mark the moment we left the
10   EU. Three years on, we returned with them to the same spot.

Sophie Clausen, Stratford4Europe: Brexit, er, has made this country a lot poorer, people a lot more (⁴   ), and, um, but no one wants to talk about it anymore.

Forsyth: Here, like in many places, the debate has (⁵   ) quietened,
15   though not disappeared. And these friends have just realized they've been on different sides throughout.

Mike Mills: I still think it was the right thing to do. A lot of people thought it was instantly going to (⁶   ) big change to the country, but it'll take time. I believe in this country.

20 **Dawn Repton:** I voted for 'leave', yeah.

Forsyth: And are, are you still sure now about the vote that you made then?

Repton: At the moment, yeah. There's been a change of parliament, change of (⁷   ). We'll just wait and see, really.

Forsyth: And how about you guys? You're, you're friends, same friendship group …

25 **Chorus:** Yeah.

Forsyth: … different view.

Andrew Osborn: I still think we should have remained. I think it's, we've, we've made a big mistake. We've (⁸   ) ourselves from our neighbours.

Forsyth: If there was another chance to do it again, or go back in, would you want
30   to?

Osborn: We respect the vote. And that's where we need to stay. Going back in now isn't an (⁹   ).

Forsyth: So, some things they do agree on.

Man: With what he's just said, we, we're still friends.

Forsyth: Brexit (ⁱ⁰   ) and divided politics and much of our national conversation for years. But soon after we actually left the European Union, the COVID pandemic swept the globe, with all the economic, social, and political (¹¹   ) that followed. Now, three years on, with some aspects of Brexit still (¹²   ), some are still trying to understand what its true (¹³   ) has been. At Stratford Bridge Club, some are waiting to see how things (¹⁴   ), but others have already changed their minds.   **35**   **40**

Judy Thomas: I'm (¹⁵   ) to say I voted for Brexit. We were obviously lied to, so much. And I just feel a fool.

Forsyth: A fool?

Thomas: (¹⁶   ) a fool. With all the people who've had to leave the country, and then you've got the lorries on the motorways. I mean, it's just, there's just so many, so many things. There's just …   **45**

Richard Shimmin: I'm finding it difficult to keep (¹⁷   ). I disagree totally with everything Judy has said. I don't believe we were lied to.

Forsyth: A long-term Conservative supporter, Richard says the government hasn't (¹⁸   ).   **50**

Forsyth: Do you feel like you've got what you voted for with Brexit?

Shimmin: Absolutely not. I mean, we were (¹⁹   ) a bonfire of EU laws. We were (²⁰   ) that we'd have our own UK Bill of Rights. If these things had happened, then I think the country would be in a totally different but better position.   **55**   **60**

Forsyth: So, years after the votes were counted, and then the country departed, it seems some of the (²¹   ) about Brexit are still playing out. Alex Forsyth, BBC News, Stratford-upon-Avon.

Notes

ℓ3 **Stratford-upon-Avon**「ストラトフォード・アポン・エイヴォン」イングランド中部のウォリックシャー州にある町。ウィリアム・シェイクスピア (William Shakespeare, 1564-1616) 生誕の地として知られている   ℓ6 **Brexit**「イギリスの EU 離脱」   ℓ11 **Stratford4 Europe**「ストラトフォード・フォー・ヨーロッパ」ストラトフォードでイギリスの EU 残留を求めて活動している組織。2016 年設立   ℓ40 **Stratford (-upon-Avon) Bridge Club**「ストラトフォード (・アポン・エイヴォン) ブリッジ・クラブ」ストラトフォードにあるブリッジを行うクラブ。ブリッジはトランプを用いて 2 対 2 の 4 人で行うカードゲーム   ℓ58 **Bill of Rights**「権利章典」

他の加盟国と EU 離脱

　イギリス（Britain）は EU 離脱（Brexit）を実行しましたが、他の加盟国も離脱（exit）と無縁ではありません。ギリシャ（Greece）は 2009 年に明らかになった財政危機に対処すべく EU に支援を要請しましたが、EU 側が条件として提示した厳しい緊縮財政政策を 2015 年の国民投票において拒否したため、EU ならびに共通通貨であるユーロ圏からの離脱（Grexit）の可能性が浮上しました。しかし、最終的にギリシャ政府が EU 案を受け入れたことで離脱は回避されました。フランス（France）でも、2017 年の大統領選において、極右政党・国民戦線（Front National）のマリオン・アンヌ・ペリーヌ・ル・ペン（Marion Anne Perrine Le Pen, 1968-　）が EU 離脱（Frexit）を問う国民投票の実施を主張し支持率を伸ばしたものの、落選という結果になりました。他にも、イタリア（Italy）の離脱（Itexit または Italexit）やスペイン（Spain）の離脱（Spexit）など、各国の EU 離脱を表す造語が登場しており、EU の基盤の揺らぎが示唆されています。

MOVING ON

Making a Summary

 CD 2-19

Fill the gaps to complete the summary.

　Brexit (**d**　　　　　　　　　) British conversation for years, until the UK left the EU in January 2020. Since then, there has been COVID and economic (**t**　　　　　　), with lots of issues still (**u**　　　　　　), so it has been hard to understand the (**i**　　　　　) of Brexit. The residents of Stratford-upon-Avon are regularly visited to (**g**　　　　　) how they feel, because in the 2016 referendum, they voted in the same way as the country: 52% to leave and 48% to remain. Some of them were not happy. They felt the country was poorer and more (**d**　　　　　). They said they had (**a**　　　　　) themselves from their neighbours, and they had been lied to, with people leaving the country and lorries stuck on the roads. Others thought Brexit was the right thing to do, but they should wait and see what (**u**　　　　　). One man complained that the UK had been promised a (**b**　　　　　) of EU laws and its own Bill of Rights. If that had happened, the UK would be better off.

Follow Up

Discuss, write or present.

1. Go onto the web and find out what we do know about the impact of Brexit. Is Britain richer? What problems has it brought?

2. As you listen to these people from Stratford-upon-Avon, do you get any impression from what they say about why the people voted to leave the EU?

3. Many people voted for Brexit because they wanted 'sovereignty'. They only wanted British laws and not laws made with other countries. Do you feel the same?

Genomes of All Life in the British Isles

現在イギリスでは、生物のゲノム解析に関する壮大な
プロジェクトが進行中です。一体どのようなものなの
でしょうか。ニュースを見てみましょう。

On Air Date   13 June 2022

STARTING OFF

Setting the Scene

What do you think?

1. What do biologists do?

2. Do you think that biology is an important science? What have biologists achieved in the past century?

3. What is DNA?

Building Language

Which word (1-6) best fits which explanation (a-f) ?

1. sequence [　]
2. bizarre [　]
3. extract [　]
4. foundation [　]
5. adapt [　]
6. endeavour [　]

a. remove or separate something from something bigger

b. make changes in order to survive in different conditions

c. arrange two or more things in the right successive order

d. extremely strange and unusual

e. an effort in order to achieve something

f. the starting point or solid basis for something

WATCHING THE NEWS

Understanding Check 1

Read the quotes, then watch the news and match them to the right people.

a. And we want to make that possible for all of biology.

b. ... it seems like a lot, but really it's er, er, just the beginning.

c. ... and how they interact with other species in their ecosystem.

d. ... in what is probably the most ambitious project ever undertaken ...

( )   ( )   ( )   ( )

Understanding Check 2

Which is the best answer?

1. Which one of the following descriptions of the situation is correct?

  a. The human genome has 200 billion letters of DNA, which is 60 times more than microalgae.

  b. There are 70,000 species of polychaetes, but biologists have only found about 120.

  c. There are 70,000 species of microalgae, and over 100 are surprising.

  d. There are 70,000 species of life in the British Isles, including about 120 species of marine worm.

2. How long can it take today to sequence the genome of one species?

  a. a few days   **b.** two decades

  c. years   **d.** until 2030

3. Why is it really important to sequence the genome of a badger? Which of the following was <u>not</u> mentioned?

  a. We want to know how they adapt to their environment.

  b. It's important to know how they interact with other species.

  c. Badgers used to be common, but have become scarce.

  d. We need to know how they adapt to diseases.

What do you remember?

4. Why do scientists want to sequence the genomes of all forms of life in the British Isles? What will be the benefits?

---

5. We heard about polychaetes and microalgae, but what other living things can you remember being mentioned?

---

6. What did Professor Mark Blaxter from the Wellcome Sanger Institute hope that their research would make possible?

Background Information

　今回のニュースは、ブリテン諸島のあらゆる生物のゲノム解析をしようとする壮大なプロジェクトの紹介となっています。このプロジェクトは「ダーウィン命の木 (Darwin Tree of Life)」という名称で、世界有数のゲノム科学研究拠点の1つであるウェルカム・サンガー研究所を中心とする共同研究です。オックスフォード大学 (University of Oxford)、ケンブリッジ大学 (University of Cambridge)、エディンバラ大学 (University of Edinburgh) の3大学をはじめ、ロンドンの自然史博物館 (The Natural History Museum)、キュー王立植物園 (The Royal Botanic Gardens, Kew) とエディンバラ王立植物園 (The Royal Botanic Garden Edinburgh)、プリマス海洋研究所 (Marine Biological Association, Plymouth) など、11の団体が参加しています。ブリテン諸島にはおよそ 70,000 の種が生息すると言われており、それらすべてをゲノム解析すべく、2019 年 11 月にプロジェクトの第 1 段階が開始され、まずは 2,000 種の解析を目指しています。

　ニュースでも言及されているとおり、ヒトゲノムの配列決定は 2003 年にウェルカム・サンガー研究所で完了しましたが、当初は DNA の断片を 1 本 1 本調べる「サンガー・シーケンス (Sanger sequencing)」という方法を用いており、ヒトの DNA に含まれる 32 億の塩基対を解読するのに 13 年を要しました。しかし、今では DNA の配列を解読する技術が驚異的な進歩を遂げたため、ヒト 1 人分の DNA 配列を調べるのはおよそ 2 日で終わります。そのため、個人の DNA 配列を調べて医療に活用することが可能になり、医学も目覚ましい発展を遂げています。現在イギリスでは、全新生児の DNA 配列を調べることも提案されていますが、コスト面のみならず、データの扱いに対する懸念から、慎重な検討が求められています。

　地球は現在、第 6 の大量絶滅に突入してしまったと考えられており、人類が生きるのに不可欠な生物多様性が危機に瀕しています。このプロジェクトは、ゲノム学を用いて生物多様性を理解し、できる限り多くの種を保存して、大惨事を回避しようとするものです。解析されたデータは開示され、他の様々な研究に利用されることが期待されています。

参考：
https://www.sanger.ac.uk/collaboration/darwin-tree-of-life-project/
https://www.nature.com/scitable/topicpage/dna-sequencing-technologies-key-to-the-human-828/
https://www.theguardian.com/news/2018/sep/21/solving-the-genome-puzzle

Filling Gaps

Watch the news, then fill the gaps in the text.

Newsreader: Now, in what is probably the most ambitious project ever undertaken in the field of biology, a team of scientists is planning to (¹   ) the genomes of all forms of life in the British Isles, estimated to be some 70,000 species. And the project could transform how we understand the natural world,
5   and there may well be (²   ) for humans, in search of medicines and materials inspired by nature. Our science editor, Rebecca Morelle, has been finding out more.

Rebecca Morelle: A close-up look at our (³   ) and wonderful natural world. From a delicate sea creature, called a brittle star, to a hermit crab,
10   carrying a sea anemone on its back; and these (⁴   ) animals, known as mud owls: all of these creatures were scooped up just off the coast of Plymouth.

Patrick Adkins, research scientist, Marine Biological Association: So you, you've got two worms here, and this one, it's, it's almost made
15   these (⁵   ) scales of kind of sandy shell.

Morelle: They are being (⁶   ) for an
20   ambitious new project: to (⁷   ) the genomes of all life in the British Isles. Today, scientists are focusing on marine worms, known as polychaetes.

Adkins: It's a big task with, with hundreds and hundreds of species, and we, we've
25   got over 100 now, I think 120-odd species of polychaetes (⁸   ). Um, er, it seems like a lot, but really, it's er, er, just the beginning.

Morelle: The plan is to (⁹   ) the DNA of every plant, animal, and fungi in Britain and Ireland. That's about 70,000 species, and some of them are surprising. There's a type of microalgae that has 200 billion (¹⁰   )
30   of DNA: that's more than 60 times bigger than the human genome, and the scientists plan to do this all by 2030.

Morelle: The DNA (¹¹   ) is being carried out at the Wellcome Sanger Institute. The human genome was (¹²   ) here two decades ago.

That took years, but now a species can be completed in a few days.

Professor Mark Blaxter, Wellcome Sanger Institute: When the human genome
was (¹³   ), it changed the way we do human biology forever. It's
really (¹⁴   ) how we see ourselves: how we work with our health
and illness. And we want to make that possible for all of biology. So we want
everybody working on any species, or any group of species anywhere in the
world, able to have this ultimate (¹⁵   ).

Morelle: One genome that is now complete belongs to the badger. In Oxfordshire,
as dusk falls, a family (¹⁶   ) from their set. Scientists say having
their detailed genetic information is vital.

Dr Tanesha Allen, zoologist, University of Oxford: Getting the badger

genome-(¹⁷   ) is
really important because we can
see how badgers
(¹⁸   ) to diseases,
how they (¹⁹   ) to
their environment, and how they
interact with other species in
their ecosystem.

Morelle: Back onshore in Plymouth, the rock pools are full of surprises, but their
genetic code could also help us to find nature-inspired medicines or materials.
This immense (²⁰   ) could change our understanding of the
(²¹   ) of life. Rebecca Morelle, BBC News, Plymouth.

Notes

ℓ3 **genomes**「ゲノム」全遺伝情報　ℓ3 **the British Isles**「ブリテン諸島」グレート・ブリテン島、アイルランド島と6,000を超える属
島の総称　ℓ9 **brittle star**「クモヒトデ」クモヒトデ網に属する棘皮動物の総称　ℓ11 **mud owls**「ダルマゴカイ」環形動物門多毛網ダルマ
ゴカイ科に属する海産動物。正式名はsternaspidae　ℓ12 **Plymouth**「プリマス」イングランド南西部デヴォン州 (Devon) にある港
湾都市　ℓ13 **Marine Biological Association**「海洋生物学協会」プリマスに拠点を置く学術団体。1884年設立　ℓ23
polychaetes「多毛類」環形動物門多毛網に属する海洋生物の総称　ℓ32 **the Wellcome Sanger Institute**「ウェルカム・サン
ガー研究所」医学の研究支援を行っているウェルカム財団 (the Wellcome Trust) からの資金提供により1992年に設立された、ゲノム
を研究する施設。ヒトの健康と疾患に関する遺伝学の世界的理解を促進している　ℓ41 **Oxfordshire**「オックスフォードシャー」イングラン
ド南東部の州　ℓ42 **set**「(アナグマの) 巣穴」

　ゲノムや DNA の研究が進んで犯罪捜査の精度がさらに高まると、迷宮入りした歴史上の事件の真相も解明されるかもしれません。19 世紀末のロンドンで娼婦たちを次々と殺した殺人鬼、切り裂きジャック (Jack the Ripper) の正体は長年の謎でしたが、2014 年、真犯人を特定したと主張する研究者が現れました。リバプール・ジョン・ムーア大学 (Liverpool John Moores University) のヤリ・ロウヘライネン (Jari Louhelainen) 博士は、被害者のショールに残っていた犯人の痕跡を最新の DNA 鑑定技術で分析した結果、DNA が容疑者の 1 人であったポーランド人理髪師のものと一致したと述べました。博士はアメリカの『法科学ジャーナル』(*Journal of Forensic Sciences*) に 2019 年に掲載された論文においても同様の結論を発表していますが、信憑性を疑う声も相次いでおり、真相はいまだに謎に包まれています。

MOVING ON

Making a Summary

 CD 2-22

Fill the gaps to complete the summary.

　　The Wellcome Sanger Institute is aiming to (**e** 　　　　　) and (**s** 　　　　　) the DNA of all 70,000 species in the British Isles. This knowledge could (**t** 　　　　　) how we work with our health and illness, and benefit us in our search for medicines and materials (**i** 　　　　　) by nature. The aim is for biologists everywhere to use this knowledge as a (**f** 　　　　　) for their work. A lot of (**w** 　　　　　) creatures have been collected, such as brittle stars, hermit crabs, and some (**b** 　　　　　) animals called mud owls. Today, scientists are focusing on polychaetes, or marine worms. They have collected about a hundred species, which is just the beginning. One animal whose genome is complete is the badger. It is important to find out how they (**a** 　　　　　) to diseases and their environment. All in all, it is an immense (**e** 　　　　　), which will help us to understand the (**d** 　　　　　) of life.

Follow Up

Discuss, write or present.

1. Search the web to find out how many animal species there are in Japan. Which are the most interesting? Are any of these species endangered?

2. The biologist wanted to give this knowledge freely to scientists all over the world. However, some people think that if companies were able to make a profit by selling their knowledge, they would discover more. What do you think?

3. The complete sequencing of the human genome was a huge achievement. However, there is a lot of concern about it. Why do you think that is?

BBCニュースは、
世界の最新情報を
24時間お届けしています。

最新ニュースはBBCニュース
日本語版でもご覧いただけます。
ww.bbc.com/japanese

現場に立ち会う
自らの足で取材する
スピードより正確さを優先する
単一の情報源に依存しない
確認し、検証する

このテキストのメインページ
www.kinsei-do.co.jp/plusmedia/419
次のページの QR コードを読み取ると
直接ページにジャンプできます

オンライン映像配信サービス「plus⁺Media」について

本テキストの映像は plus⁺Media ページ（www.kinsei-do.co.jp/plusmedia）から、ストリーミング再生でご利用いただけます。手順は以下に従ってください。

ログイン

ログインページ

●ご利用には、ログインが必要です。
　サイトのログインページ（www.kinsei-do.co.jp/plusmedia/login）へ行き、plus⁺Media パスワード（次のページのシールをはがしたあとに印字されている数字とアルファベット）を入力します。

●パスワードは各テキストにつき1つです。
　有効期限は、<u>はじめてログインした時点から1年間</u>になります。

[利用方法]

次のページにある QR コード、もしくは plus⁺Media トップページ（www.kinsei-do.co.jp/plusmedia）から該当するテキストを選んで、そのテキストのメインページにジャンプしてください。

メニューページ　　　再生画面

plus+Media トップ　　　メインページ

「Video」「Audio」をタッチすると、それぞれのメニューページにジャンプしますので、そこから該当する項目を選べば、ストリーミングが開始されます。

[推奨環境]

iOS (iPhone, iPad)	OS: iOS 12 以降 ブラウザ：標準ブラウザ	Android	OS: Android 6 以降 ブラウザ：標準ブラウザ、Chrome
PC	OS: Windows 7/8/8.1/10, MacOS X　ブラウザ: Internet Explorer 10/11, Microsoft Edge, Firefox 48以降, Chrome 53以降, Safari		

※最新の推奨環境についてはウェブサイトをご確認ください。
※上記の推奨環境を満たしている場合でも、機種によってはご利用いただけない場合もあります。また、推奨環境は技術動向等により変更される場合があります。予めご了承ください。

▲ここからはがして下さい

このシールをはがすと
plus+Media 利用のための
パスワードが
記載されています。

一度はがすと元に戻すことは
できませんのでご注意下さい。

4191 British News
Update 6
(BBC)

plus+Media®

本書にはCD（別売）があります

British News Update 6

映像で学ぶ　イギリス公共放送の最新ニュース6

2024年1月20日　初版第1刷発行
2024年8月30日　初版第3刷発行

編著者　Timothy Knowles

田　中　みんね

中　村　美帆子

馬　上　紗矢香

発行者　福　岡　正　人

発行所　　株式会社　金　星　堂

（〒101-0051）東京都千代田区神田神保町 3-21
Tel. (03)3263-3828（営業部）
(03)3263-3997（編集部）
Fax (03)3263-0716
https://www.kinsei-do.co.jp

編集担当　戸田浩平　　　　　　　　　　　Printed in Japan
印刷所・製本所／三美印刷株式会社

ISBN978-4-7647-4191-1 C1082